All Hat and No Cattle

All Hat and No Cattle

TALES OF A
CORPORATE OUTLAW

How to Shake Things Up and
Make a Difference at Work

CHRIS TURNER

Foreword by Alan Webber,
Founding Editor, *Fast Company*

PERSEUS BOOKS
Cambridge, Massachusetts

Many of the designations used by manufacturers and sellers to distinguish their products are claimed as trademarks. Where those designations appear in this book and Perseus Books was aware of a trademark claim, the designations have been printed in initial capital letters.

Library of Congress Catalog Card Number: 99-65901

ISBN: 0-7382-0096-4

Copyright © 1999 by Chris Turner

For more information on overcoming corporate complacency and creating real change in organizations, please visit the World Wide Web at http://www.corporateoutlaw.com.

Perseus Books is a member of the Perseus Books Group.

Jacket design by Bruce W. Bond
Text design by Heather Hutchison
Set in 11-point Stone Serif

2 3 4 5 6 7 8 9 10—03 02 01 00
First printing, August 1999

Perseus Books are available at special discounts for bulk purchases in the United States by corporations, institutions, and other organizations. For more information, please contact the Special Markets Department at HarperCollins Publishers, 10 East 53rd Street, New York, NY 10022, or call 1–212–207–7528.

Find us on the World Wide Web at http://www.perseusbooks.com.

For Tracy and Chip
My children
My teachers

Contents

Foreword

Chris Turner is the real deal.

We've all picked up business books written by academics who are trying to impress us with their research and theory. We've all picked up business books written by consultants (or purported to be written by them anyway) trying to impress us with their clients and models. And we've all picked up business books written by "great communicators" trying to impress us with their wit and wisdom.

You have just picked up a book written by a real businessperson. A book written by a real change agent. A book written by a real learning person. A book written by a real Texan—hell, she's so real, she even writes with a twang!

The fact is, we've just spent the last ten years or more trying to figure out how to get big, slow companies to change. First came a wave of financial reengineering. The idea was to take the big companies apart—break off the different pieces, unleash the pent-up economic value, and make big companies operate more entrepreneurially. It turned out that stripping out assets made Wall Street deal makers very wealthy, but it didn't make big, slow companies any faster. After financial engineering failed to work, the next round was just plain reengineering. The idea was to redesign the big companies from scratch, to reorganize the business processes, streamline the operations, and make big companies operate more entrepreneurially. It turned out that outsourcing, downsizing, and laying off people made management consultants very wealthy, but didn't make big, slow companies any faster. More recently a variety of smaller ideas have flourished: mergers and acquisitions (putting all the old pieces back together again); overlaying new software systems on top of the existing business processes (reengineering the reengineering); and forgetting about the old game and just throwing everything at the Web and seeing what sticks.

Now along comes li'l ol' Chris Turner. Chris Turner who's just an aw-shucks good ol' gal. Chris Turner who's not trying to sell you any fancy business model or management theory. But also Chris Turner who's lived in the belly of the beast at Xerox, who's seen what makes big, slow companies act big and slow, and who's been remarkably effective as a change agent in getting a big, slow company to discover its own capacity to operate with a different clock speed and a different bandwidth.

And she's got it pretty much right. The reason all those big company efforts at change failed was because they had it all wrong. And the really sad part is that they lacked not only the fundamental understanding of what it would take to change a big company, but also the underlying respect for the people they worked with, the purposes of the work that the people were engaged in, and the values of the people who take their work lives seriously. When we stop long enough to be honest about it, we see that the problem is that the change programs of the past lacked basic integrity. They were cynical—and people inside any organization can smell cynicism a mile away.

Now, the need to change is the one thing that hasn't changed. Even after all the cookbook change methods have failed, big, slow companies still have a problem: The world of work is undergoing radical, rapid reinvention. The rules of work, of competition, of engagement are all changing. The technology is changing. The boundaries are changing. The generations are changing. And companies must be about the work of changing. So Chris is offering you her approach to change, an approach based on her experience, rooted in her values, grounded in her character. And the fact that what she has to say is so simple and honest and true that we all immediately know that she's right doesn't make it any easier—it just means that we all know she's right, and now we've really got our work cut out for us.

What she tells us requires the hardest kinds of change: It requires us to change how we think about all the things that we do at work. It requires us to change how we think about all the things that made us successful for so long. It requires us to look at ourselves first—and you know how hard that is—and discover long-submerged truths about the human heart.

So what is she telling us? If you want to change your big, slow company, you can't drive change, you've got to disturb the system. Once you hear it, you immediately know that it's right: Companies aren't machines, they're living systems. You can't change a company's culture the way you change a car's spark plug. You have to interact with a company the way you interact with any living system. You disturb it. You poke at it or you joke with it. You change its diet or you alter its location. You check its emotions, and you introduce new notions. And as you disturb the system, the system discovers that it has no choice but to change. It shifts in order to accommodate the new information it's getting about its condition and keeps shifting as you keep changing its flow of information. That's why Chris was Xerox's "chief learning person"—because she was teaching the company's whole system how to interpret its new circumstances, how to accommodate the new world of competition, and how to adapt to all that new information.

The second big idea that Chris has to offer is just as revolutionary. If you want to make change happen, you have to embrace love-based management systems. Now, coming from some people, that's the kind of idea that you could easily dismiss as New Age tree-huggery. But not when it comes from Chris. She's spent too many years out-working, out-hustling, out-thinking, and, when necessary, out-drinking the competition for anyone to think that underneath those cowboy boots, she's wearing a pair of leg warmers. But what she's grasped is an essential fact of life in the new economy: You can't get people to make an exceptional commitment to sustained great performances out of fear. Threats and intimidation, mind games and manipulations just won't work. The only way to get people to achieve remarkable results is by being willing to show them that you genuinely and personally care about them.

Which leads us to Chris's third big idea: It's the people, stupid! Working in a big, proud hardware and technology operation, Chris had a chance to see firsthand the new rules of business. Those new rules make it very clear that as important as technology, hardware, financial strength, brand-name awareness, distribution channels, and all the rest are in competition today, rule number one is this: The team with the best people wins. Period. Everything else is table stakes. Everything else is fungible—anyone can more or less match you, item by item. The only basis for winning in business is people: You want to win? Get more than your fair share of the best talent.

Of course, there's a corollary: It's the leadership, stupid! These days, exceptionally talented people don't work for a company—they work for a person they respect, admire, and hope to learn from. They work for a person who treats them with honesty, respect, and integrity, a person willing to learn and listen regardless of position, a person open to new ideas.

In other words, talented people gravitate toward a truth-teller in the world of business, where, all too often, dishonesty, ego, distortion, and lies are the norm. The stories that Chris tells and the lessons she draws from her own experiences make it unmistakably clear that we are entering a new world of work, and that leaders of once-great and once-successful companies have to be the first to change their ways if, in turn, they hope to lead change in their organizations. At the same time, it's up to the rest of us to be unafraid and unrelenting change agents in the interests of creating the kinds of workplaces that are not only successful, but also humane.

Now, as soon as you read this, you know that it's true. You know that it makes sense. You know that it's right. And you know that Chris has nailed both what's wrong with most organizations and what it will take to set them right.

I knew it the first time I met her. I had gone to Rochester to interview Chris for an article for *Fast Company*. After we sat down to do the interview, she instantly changed the context, first from an interview to a conversation, and then from a conversation to a friendship. Looking back on that first meeting, more than two years ago, and now, having read her book, I can tell you that all she was doing was practicing what she preaches: She was disturbing the system, creating a relationship of mutual respect, banishing fear from the room, and entertaining an openness to new thinking, new ideas, and new directions. She was telling me in her own, original, down-to-earth fashion that these are the truths that will set you free.

And you know what? She's right.

Which is why I tell you, Chris Turner is the real deal.

Alan M. Webber
Fast Company *magazine*

Acknowledgments

I could not have written *All Hat and No Cattle* without the support of a great many people. My family, with its wicked sense of humor and tweaked view of reality, has helped me, as always, keep things in perspective. I'm particularly grateful to my son, Chip, who has endured hours of listening to me think out loud and has paid me back in full for all the years I critiqued his writing. Tracy, my daughter, has kept me entertained with trenchant commentary on affairs in the great state of Texas and beyond. Only she would describe Disney World as "so nauseatingly cheerful and perfect that even the bird poop is shaped like Mickey Mouse." My brother, Alex Clarke, while teasing me unmercifully, has handled our seemingly endless family affairs so that I could finish this book. My aunts, Edna Doyle and Joyce Johnson, holders of our family memory, continually inspire me with their wisdom, grit, and love of life.

I also want to thank friends: Ann Perle for insisting that my next step was to write a book; Wes Smith, who helped me navigate the publishing world and coached me through the writing process; Dana Burch, who read the manuscript and, in the course of many long and rambling conversations, enriched my ideas about the convergence of business and ethics; Electra Carlin, who has been a mentor and second mother for many years; members of our Maturana circle, whose observations and commentary expanded and deepened my thinking; and, finally, my childhood pals who constantly remind me that true humor lies not in jokes but in everyday life.

At Xerox Business Services (XBS), it took many people to bring our broad, amorphous strategy into being. Diane Phillips, Diane Thielfoldt, and Lynn Robisch Hay worked tirelessly and energetically to make things happen and to support the widely distributed XBS community. Their patience, laughter, intelligence, imagination, and courage under fire were awesome. And thanks to Carole Webber, who with humor, tenacity, and very little money fought an uphill battle to integrate our approaches into Rank Xerox. Norm Rickard gets my thanks, because he had been a change agent himself and was understanding, compassionate, and supportive—even when I drove him crazy. And John Cooney, who had the dubious pleasure of managing me for four years, was wonderfully encouraging. I also want to thank the Partners in Lur'ning, who integrated our approaches into the field organization; the Learning Centers—San Antonio, Denver, and Seattle—for allowing us to use them as guinea pigs; and to all the outside partners—especially IRL—who helped us in more ways than I can mention. And finally, thanks to my buddies who helped me survive corporate life by teaching me to laugh when it hurts. You know who you are.

I'm grateful to Alan Webber, who recognized what was going on at XBS and wrote about it in *Fast Company*. And, of course, muchas gracias to my agent, Rafe Sagalyn, who encouraged me to write from a Texan's point of view. Thanks also to Nick Philipson, my editor at Perseus, whose immense good humor and gentle approach encouraged me to get back to writing after a big personal loss; and Stephanie Vander Weide, who helped a first-timer wind her way through the publisher's labyrinth.

All Hat and No Cattle

1

All Hat and No Cattle

Loyalty to a petrified opinion never yet broke a chain or
freed a human soul.

Mark Twain

My family never did hold much with organized religion. The
fact is, we ended up in Texas because my great-grandfather
roughed up a priest in Arkansas. Seems the good father didn't
want to bury a nonbaptized child in the Catholic cemetery,
and my great-granddaddy took offense at such malarkey. Anyway, he was run out of town and made his way to Texas, for
which I am eternally grateful, as I would sure rather be from
Texas than from Arkansas any day of the week.

Given this background you'll understand how I came by my
habit of challenging rules and dogma. Questioning the status
quo is something I have done all my life, so it was pretty hard
working in a large corporate bureaucracy for sixteen years. I
wouldn't have done it at all except I really needed the money.

I mean, I had gone to college—although, truth be known,
my blood alcohol content was higher than my grade-point average. And I even had succeeded in some pretty cool public re-
lations jobs in Fort Worth. But these gigs surely weren't
supporting me in the style to which I was accustomed; so in

1981 I concluded that it was time to grow up and get a real job, one that required more chutzpah than academic success.

I interviewed several times with Xerox, and the company appeared to fill the bill. From what I could gather, at Xerox energy was a lot more important than book learning, so I figured I had a shot at doing really well. My final interview was with the general manager, who posed a bunch of standard questions before surprising me by asking about the most immature thing I had ever done. Without thinking I said, "Oh, marrying someone because he was a good dancer." He fell off his chair laughing, and I wasn't sure if that was good or bad. He later said that he hired me because I had a sense of humor and that I was going to need it.

What quickly became clear is that Xerox offered great potential for rule breaking, because nothing could ever get done otherwise. It was also apparent that this place was passing strange. Although people were fairly buttoned down and saw themselves as part of a real professional outfit, I was surprised at what a mess the place was. And the language was so weird that it was a couple of weeks before I figured out that everyone wasn't speaking in tongues. Nope, Xerox had a language of its own. I tried to learn the lingo as soon as possible because it was clearly important to fit in.

In fact, these became my guides for survival—walk and talk like a Xeroid and don't let rules get in the way. I also realized that you had to suspend all rational thought. And I did OK. After being a sales rep for a couple of years, I became a sales manager, then a marketing manager, and in 1987, I moved to Pennsylvania as general manager of the Pittsburgh operation for Xerox Business Services (XBS). XBS is the outsourcing arm of Xerox and offers complete document services to large businesses, law firms, and educational institutions. Customer contracts include all staffing, all supplies, all hardware, and all software required to produce the customer's information—either in digital or paper form. Most of Pittsburgh's 150 XBSers worked at customer accounts throughout western Pennsylvania.

But no matter what job I was doing, I spent most of my time trying to climb out of the quagmire of organizational non-sense. In one frustrated conversation with my dad, who had spent years with a large oil company, we agreed that the wonder is that any of these damn corporations survive at all. He told me about a new purchasing procedure in his company that required petroleum engineers to bid out oil well repair work. In the oil patch, obviously, the most important thing is to keep the black gold flowing—especially back in the early 1980s, when a barrel of oil cost more than a quart of Pellegrino water. You don't want to waste time bidding out every repair. I asked Dad how he was dealing with this procedure. He laughed, "Well, the rule states that if something goes wrong on the weekend, you don't have to bid out the job. In West Texas everything breaks on the weekend."

I found jobs at Xerox consuming and frustrating for lots of reasons. First of all, the place was so political that to stay alive, I had to spend considerable time figuring out who could hurt me the least when I ticked them off. No matter what I did, it teed someone off. Either I made the bigwigs happy by working folks to death, or I made our operation's people happy by refusing to jump through hoops on the latest headquarters initiative. The decision depended on lots of factors—sometimes on something as absurd as whether it was time for my performance appraisal or time for the latest employee satisfaction survey.

The internal demands were so <u>onerous</u> that it was often tough to get out and see customers. During the first quarter of the

onerous: Causing hardship, troublesome, burdensome.

year, managers had to schedule kickoff meetings, introduce a bunch of new headquarters programs, write performance reviews for the previous year, write performance objectives for the coming year, write multiple marketing plans and action plans, and respond to the usual heavy headquarters requests for information. Then, of course, when the business went south in the first three months, we had to answer for that. "You mean you haven't spent at least three days a week with customers?" the big feet would ask. Once, in a fit of frustration, I presented my boss with a list of everything on my plate and asked him which thing he wanted me to do first. "All of them," he sputtered.

In 1992, I finally took a job in XBS's Rochester headquarters to see if I could help change things. Talk about going from the frying pan into the fire. I was executive assistant to the president, Curt Stiles. Curt was a former Marine—and I quickly realized that there is no such thing. Fortunately, after the longest nine months of my life, we reorganized. In 1993, I became part of the XBS Quality group and was asked to figure out an "empowerment strategy." Thank you, Jesus! The fox is in charge of the henhouse! I spent the next four years experimenting with an unconventional approach to change and stewing about why organizations are such a mess.

And here is the dirty little secret: All hat and no cattle. It Texas, that's how we describe anything that is all style and no substance. All hat and no cattle is corporate America's managerial archetype. Sure, there are lots of smart people and a handful of original thinkers—and some of these folks manage to withstand having all their ideas and creativity beat out of them. But many of the best and brightest get weeded out before reaching executive jobs.

All hat and no cattle is a way of life—not just in Xerox, but clear across the business landscape. There is a scarcity of deep thinking, of challenging the way things are, of fresh ideas. Management teams too often are made up of people who think, walk, and talk alike; who spend more time worrying about stock price than the quality and depth of organizational thinking; and who spend little time on personal learning, exploring new ideas, or expanding their worldviews. Ideas that challenge the status quo are usually dismissed out of hand. The old, stale thinking of these teams seeps into organizational systems, creating environments that are, for the most part, sluggish, mediocre, and damn near unconscious.

I recently talked to a friend in a Fortune 50 company who was assigned to a team chartered to downsize the company—a team headed up by the vice president of Human Resources. Depressed team members dragged into meetings as if they were going to their own executions. Their moods were not helped by the good ol' boy veep who, from time to time, surveyed the room and opined, "We are doing the Lord's work."

Another friend recounted his recent conversation with a senior manager—rumored as the soon-to-be "pick of the litter" for a corporate vice presidency—who described one peer as having a tough "fah cod." It took a few minutes for my friend to realize the guy meant *facade*.

Yep, those are the smart ones running the show—and they hire in their own images. No wonder things are such a mess. I've puzzled about the mediocrity of some corporate chieftains, wondering how this pattern perpetuates itself in so many places. A story from William Langewiesche's book, *Inside the Sky*, illuminates the phenomenon. Langewiesche dedicates one chapter to the crash of Valujet 592 and describes how the head of the Federal Aviation Administration (FAA) reacted to the tragedy:

facade? fancy house front.

The FAA's administrator then was a one-time airline boss named David Hinson, the sort of glib and self-assured executive who does well in closed circles of like-minded men. Now, however, he would have to address a diverse and skeptical audience. The day after the Valujet accident he had flown to Miami and made the incredible assertion that Valujet was a safe airline—when for 110 people lying dead in a nearby swamp it very obviously was not. He also said, "I would fly on it," as if he believed he had to reassure a nation of children. It was an insulting performance, and it was taken as further evidence of the FAA's isolation and its betrayal of the public's trust. After a good night's sleep Hinson might have tried to repair the damage. Instead he appeared two days later at a Senate hearing in Washington sounding like an unrepentant Prussian: "We have a very professional, highly dedicated, organized and efficient workforce that do their job day in and day out. And when we say an airline is safe to fly, it is safe to fly. There is no gray area."

These paragraphs crystallize what I mean by all hat and no cattle. Although Hinson pretended that the Valujet crash was an anomaly, the truth was that the FAA inspectors were quite troubled about Valujet and were on the verge of grounding the airline prior to the accident. Hinson was so accustomed to operating in "closed circles of like-minded men" that he may have confused his personal worldview with reality. He either lied or developed amnesia regarding FAA concerns about Valujet when he pronounced it a safe airline. He could have been so accustomed to having his views go unchallenged that he figured he could bluff his way through one more time. *This is our story and we're sticking to it.* Or he may have believed that if he declared Valujet safe, his very words made it so. Hinson ended up denigrating the intelligence of his listeners. He assumed the patriarchal role natural to many "suits," assuring the uneducated masses, "I would fly on it." He then added insult to injury by declaring that "when we say an airline is safe to fly, then it is safe to fly. There is no gray area." Langewiesche, a pilot himself, comments that "aviation safety is nothing but gray area." The only good news in this tale is that Hinson, who could be an all-hat-and-no-cattle poster boy, ultimately lost his job.

The phrase I find particularly descriptive is "the sort of self-assured executive who does well in closed circles of like-minded men." These words could easily be applied to many corporate types—men and women. The glibness, the cockiness, the conviction that a few insiders have some special insight into "truth" are hogwash. Too often, people who want to get ahead or be part of the in crowd begin to adopt the broadly held, tired assumptions as their own. They don't challenge the organizational worldview. So all-hat-and-no-cattle thinking is perpetuated and assumes a life of its own.

Sometimes a tragedy like the Valujet crash provokes deep questioning. Other times it sends technocrats scurrying for numbers to prove they did nothing wrong and to justify the current modus operandi. Most institutional systems are self-absorbed, selecting facts that support collective beliefs, rejecting information that challenges "the way we do things here." All hat and no cattle is this self-justifying, self-perpetuating institutional habit.

What all hat and no cattle is *not* is self-interrogating. It thinks it is self-critical, but it isn't. The entire environment created by all hat and no cattle limits the playing field in terms of the questions that can be asked. Much is "undiscussible," and the fact that certain things are off limits for questioning is "undiscussible." Although folks fool themselves into believing they are asking tough questions like "how are you

going to measure it?" these questions offer little critical thinking or probing of the assumptions underlying the beliefs. All
hat and no cattle perpetuates the status quo.

Xerox fell prey to all hat and no cattle in the late seventies
and early eighties. Having had a lengthy market monopoly, the
mind-set became "We're Xerox, and customers will buy from us
no matter what kind of machines we make and what price we
charge." Then, when the market went Dixie because the Japan-
ese could sell equipment cheaper than Xerox could manufac-
ture it, the caca hit the fan. People at Xerox woke up, and since
then, the mind-set has become "We've got to get better and better and cheaper and cheaper if we are to survive." This is not to
say that the all-hat-and-no-cattle attitude does not exist at Xerox. It surely does, but not in connection with the need for
marketplace vigilance and continuous improvement.

Everyone agrees that we are living in a world of increasing
complexity, information overload, and technological revolution. There is broad agreement that to be successful in the future, institutions must rethink themselves. But beyond the
talk, there is little progress, because change comes with doing
things differently—and doing things differently starts with
thinking differently.

Enterprises have poured buckets of money into change initiatives. However, although we say we want empowerment,
learning, and innovation, our approaches are antithetical to
what we say we're after. For the most part, change is implemented in ways that are hierarchical, stale, and dreary because
"that's the way we do things here."

This mile-wide and inch-deep mentality is killing us. We
can't make progress without challenging our most deeply held
assumptions. We can only move ahead by stepping back, sus-
pending beliefs and disbeliefs, beginning with a clean slate,

and imagining the possibilities of new thinking. We must enter a new threshold of consciousness.

In the future, survival of the fittest may translate to survival of the deepest—meaning that only those who can challenge same-old, same-old thinking will be able to transcend the challenges facing us all. The opposite of all-hat-and-no-cattle thinking is thinking with integrity. And the only thinking that has integrity is that which encourages rigorous, dispassionate interrogation.

I don't know who actually said "Insanity is doing the same things over and over again and expecting different results." I have seen it attributed to everyone from Einstein to that prolific and brilliant thinker Anon. Our thinking is so dadgummed important because it is the basis for what we do. Buddha said, "We are what we think. All that we are arises with our thoughts. With our thoughts we make the world." My friend Brian Arthur, an economist at Santa Fe Institute, has a great example of how thinking affects action. He says the difference in Folgers and Starbucks is the way they each thought about coffee. Folgers thought about coffee as a commodity; Starbucks thought of it as latte, mocha, espresso—and, most important, as an experience.

Change doesn't happen from talking about it. Change happens when we think about things in new ways and then do things in new ways. And that is what this book is about—new ways of thinking and new ways of doing. Change happens in the doing, but it starts with the thinking. And, as the writer Richard Pascale points out, it is sometimes easier to act ourselves into new ways of thinking than to think ourselves into new ways of acting.

What follows is a series of chapters that challenge all hat and no cattle and outline new ways of designing initiatives, of

creating learning environments, of communicating. I will outline approaches that can be used throughout organizations
and ways that each person can shake up the system. It is written for all of you who want to kick up dust because you can
no longer stand things the way they are. It will help you spot
all-hat-and-no-cattle thinking and will suggest actions you can
take to create the kind of workplace you want.

Actions I can take? But I am just one person. Right. One example of all-hat-and-no-cattle thinking is that change is up to
"the suits," that if the execs aren't on board nothing will happen, and that individuals can't make a difference. Change is
everyone's responsibility. The kind of change called for now is
social change—change that will overthrow the two-hundred-
year-old industrial mind-set that treated the people of organizations like so many cogs inside giant machines.

Social change rarely starts at the top. It starts when people
get fed up and take responsibility for making a difference.
Think about civil rights, women's rights, environmentalism,
gun control, and antismoking laws. All these movements
started outside the establishment, not inside. So if you are
waiting for your organizational "establishment" to come to its
senses, you may wait till the cows come home.

This book is about how we begin creating the workplaces we
want, the future we want, here and now. What goes on in organizations is that we talk about the future as if it were some
faraway place—and we act that way too. "Yeah, someday we
want to be a learning organization, but we don't have time
right now." "Communication is horrible around here; someday we need to figure out what to do about it." What we've
got is "future never" organizations, and what we need are "future now" organizations.

You will begin creating the future now by communicating in new ways; understanding the organization as a complex, dynamic system; understanding how people learn; fostering environments that nurture learning; and recognizing that fundamental change happens not through official programs, but moment to moment—in every minute of every day. You will be able to create a future-now workplace and you'll understand how all hat and no cattle got a mortal lock on the organizational psyche, why it's so corrosive, and what steps you can take to make a difference. In Mark Twain's words, "The problem with most folks is that they know too much that ain't so." That's what all hat and no cattle is—stuff that ain't so.

2

We Gotta Drive
This Sucker

May God us keep
from single vision and Newton's sleep.
William Blake

Not long ago in a large Fortune 50 division, a team of top
marketing folks, division vice presidents, and sales managers
got together to try to solve a big problem. Once the "glory
boys" of the corporation, these were the guys who pulled the
fat out of the fire every December, thereby guaranteeing the
corporate bigwigs another round of obscene bonuses. But
now, this bunch had fallen on hard times. Yearly changes in
the division's management team, new compensation, new
training programs, and countless reorganizations had done
nothing to make things better—in fact, things were going
down the toilet.

The division president, trying to be as inspirational as his
hero Ross Perot, exhorted, "We just gotta get under the hood
and fix it. We gotta look at every nut and bolt and throw out
the bad parts. We gotta turn this place back into the well-oiled
machine it used to be. We gotta figure out what we were doing

that we aren't doing anymore and start doing it again. We gotta drive this sucker."

The person who told me this story was trying to help the team figure out "what we were doing that we aren't doing anymore." I had to bite my tongue to keep from saying, "Maybe nothing."

See, everyone trying to "fix" this division was making a very interesting set of assumptions—all based on the four-hundred-year-old worldview developed by Copernicus, Galileo, Descartes, Newton, Comte, and others. These men saw the world as a highly predictable machine governed by precise mathematical laws. They believed that validity was dependent on measurement and quantification. Descartes, known as the father of the scientific method, saw mind and matter as separate realms—and never the twain shall meet. This separation of mind and matter gave rise to the notion of an objective reality, one that could be understood through analysis and dissection.

Now, these were revolutionary and brilliant ideas for their time and continue to inform scientific thought. But although there have been insightful new theories in the intervening centuries—ideas that expand and deepen our understanding of the universe—today's institutions remain mired in the mechanistic, reductionist mind-set of the scientific method. The scientific method, rooted in Descartes, Newton, and the rest and brought fully into the business context by Frederick Taylor, is the basis of Total Quality Management, with its linear view and worship of quantification.

The assumptions made by the Ross Perot wannabe were as follows:

- That the organization is a machine
- That the organization can be fixed by tinkering with the parts

• That things can be like they used to be
• That they were once doing something right
• That an organization can be driven

The truth of the matter is that back in "the good old days," these good ol' boys could walk through a swamp and not get their feet muddy. Their products sold themselves. There was no competition, everyone made a lot of money, and a whole mythology grew up around this success. Marketing people were gods who won glamorous trips and got promoted. Life was good.

This company doesn't have any corner on ignorance, however. Nope, go to any number of companies, and you will find the same assumptions. Despite all the books written on complexity theory and organizations as natural, self-organizing systems, the machine mind-set is firmly in place. And this all-hat-and-no-cattle thinking limits us. It keeps us from understanding deep organizational structures and the thinking that gives rise to those structures.

When I first moved into the Quality organization in 1993, I was charged with developing an empowerment strategy. Xerox Business Services, like most organizations, thought about empowerment in a rather small way. As I became acquainted with managers from other Xerox divisions and understood their strategies, I found them to be focused primarily on self-managed teams, an approach that seemed like employee involvement dressed in drag. They were using traditional Xerox tactics—manuals filled with PowerPoint slides and a tell-tell-tell training design.

I could uncover nothing fresh or original in any of these ideas; in fact, all appeared to be based on driving and directing their enterprises. I struggled with this notion of "driving the organization," with the idea that corporate approaches must be linear, with the obsession on measurement that assumes cause and effect, and with the need for neat and tidy answers. None of this jibed with the way I saw things happening in XBS or with the challenges we faced.

At that point, we had approximately eight thousand people spread all over the world—I say "approximately" because, despite our fixation on quantification and measurement, we never could figure out exactly how many employees we had. In the United States alone there were hundreds of offices and thousands of customer sites. Because XBS is in the outsourcing business, 80 percent of its people work at customer locations.

Our only experience with planned culture change was Xerox's introduction of Leadership Through Quality ("Quality" for short), an effort I remembered all too well. At that time I was general manager in the Pittsburgh operation. As part of Leadership Through Quality, each person in the corporation was required to attend four days of training. Because customer sites had to be staffed during the week, we conducted training on weekends and, to save money, held the sessions in the basement of our operation. People dragged in, having just completed a full workweek, to be dipped in "quality dogma."

The entire effort was top down. The assumption was that, to be successful, the mandated training must be "cascaded," with each level of management receiving training prior to those at lower levels. Once the workforce was trained, participation in Quality teams became part of everyone's performance criteria. In other words, Quality was shoved down our throats.

Now I would be the first to say that Quality made a big difference in Xerox. The culture became more polite and far more disciplined in analyzing problems. The approach was particularly helpful in manufacturing, where the contained environment supported standardized approaches. Quality was a major factor in Xerox's marketplace turnaround. Xerox won the

1989 Baldrige Award, garnering glory and additional business in the process.

But what nobody at Xerox will 'fess up to is the Dark Side of Quality. First, although one objective was to create a more participatory culture, the top-down implementation reminded me of the sign in *Animal Farm:* "All animals are equal; but some animals are more equal than others." The whole shebang was hierarchical.

Second, the strategy was rooted in command and control. In a mandated approach, all the energy goes into pushing and resisting. At Xerox, there was an underlying resentment at the way Quality was forced on people. After a rah-rah presentation to a bunch of senior dweebs, one veep was overheard muttering, "I'll put on a good act, but I'm not doing this shit." And in fact, lots of effort went into creating smoke screens to convince the muckety-mucks that Quality was being used when the reality was "same old, same old."

Third, although Xerox continued to talk about valuing diversity, the tacit message in Leadership through Quality was "You can look different, even be a different gender, as long as you talk, think, and act like everyone else."

Fourth, the big cheeses didn't do Quality. Yeah, there were teamwork days to recognize good group efforts, but in their own day-to-day work, most senior managers didn't do the things they told everyone else to do. One corporate guy was famous for reacting to bad news by pounding the table and yelling, "Whose ass can I fire for this?" And this is the big weakness in top-down strategies. If there is a disjoint between what the bigwigs say and what they do, then what you immediately get is cynicism.

Fifth, the culture became obsessed with quantitative measurement. In fact, when the Institute for Research on Learning, an organization dedicated to the study of social learning, conducted an ethnographic study at XBS, the anthropologists noted that in every culture there are questions that sound reasonable but are actually hostile. They observed that in the Xerox culture, one of the hostile questions is "How are you going to measure it?"

Sixth, because the approach was mandated, the only way to get ongoing compliance was through constant inspection. So Xerox created a large Quality organization whose job was to police the joint. Of course, this was a darn near impossible assignment. As one wonk often said, "Trying to get Xerox managers to do Quality is like trying to herd cockroaches."

Seventh, Quality was regarded as the ultimate truth, an ideology that was the be-all and end-all. The "true believers" laced their conversations with Quality orthodoxy that was nauseating. One evangelist, for example, used the word "process" as other people use "uh." His random interjection of the term into conversation resulted in gibberish. Another fellow continually chanted the mantra "It's not the management of quality; it's the quality of management." Each time he said it, he looked around expectantly as if waiting for everyone to swoon.

The Leadership Through Quality effort was based on a mechanistic model, on driving and directing the system. So mechanistic approaches can be successful at some level—but at what cost?

I made a list of other strategies that had been developed and announced with fanfare only to evaporate quickly into the ether. I also calculated the money wasted on these efforts. I was convinced that there had to be an easier way. Using ideas gleaned from complexity and quantum theory as well as insights from new biology, I outlined a strategy designed not to drive the system, but to disturb it.

Dictionaries define the verb *disturb* as "to agitate, to unsettle, to cause a commotion." I set out to unsettle the system. In his essay "Circles," Emerson aptly describes the nature of disturbance:

> I unsettle all things. No facts to me are sacred; none are profane.
> I simply experiment, an endless seeker with no path at my back.

Organizational disturbances should unsettle, cause a commotion, create a ruckus, shake things up. Designed well, they lead to new thinking, to new doing, to questioning the status quo, and give rise to a new threshold of consciousness. Good disturbances create the future now.

I couldn't extricate empowerment or learning from the context of the organization. Rather, they were outcomes of the organizational environment. So the strategy focused on creating an environment where learning and empowerment flourish. Because we aimed to create a new kind of enterprise and recognized that community and character are twin-born, the disturbances were of two types: disturbances that focused on the individual and large systemic disturbances that focused primarily on new ways of doing. Although there are overlaps, it is worth drawing the distinction between individual and systemic disturbances.

We create our world and it creates us. As we change individually, the world we create daily also changes. So the idea was to expose individuals to experiences that would cause them to question their own assumptions and beliefs about "the way things are." We all love to blame others for the state of the world. As a result, it is sometimes uncomfortable to realize that each of us has a hand in creating our communities, our workplaces, and our government, and that if we don't like the way things are, we need to get off our behinds and do something.

Just as humans are living systems, so are organizations—if for no other reason than they've got people in them. Enterprises are like the environment, or the weather, or the economy. Natural systems look like this; they are open, interactive, complex, adaptive, self-organizing, nonlinear, dynamic, emergent, and playful.

Natural systems are unpredictable. Those who study complex adaptive systems counsel that we abandon our search for scientific prediction and settle for educated guesses around potential scenarios. Anyone who has participated in the ups and downs of the stock market—another natural system—understands that playing the market is more akin to shooting craps than to the scientific method.

Natural systems are self-creating and infinite. They change and move constantly. Nothing is the same from day to day. In one discussion about the XBS change strategy, a senior manager asked me how we would know when we were "there." I reminded him of what we all deeply know—that there is no "there."

The old apocryphal story about the butterfly that waves its wings in Hong Kong and changes the weather in Bermuda creates a picture of how change happens in large systems. Small disturbances can sometimes alter things in surprising and unexpected ways.

That doesn't mean that we should agitate willy-nilly. It means we must plan disturbances mindfully.

The first underlying principle of the XBS strategy was to disturb the system simultaneously all over the place—in big ways and small, individually and collectively.

The second was to disturb it in ways congruent with the kind of organization we wanted to create.

The third was to invite participation, not to insist or force it.

The fourth was to design many offerings so that people could choose how to participate.

The fifth was to keep the strategy loose, improvisational, and experimental so that we could learn along the way.

The sixth was to go to fertile ground—to offer our help and support to people who really wanted it—not to push ideas on people who weren't receptive. As a colleague of mine once said, "You can't grow grass on concrete."

The seventh principle recognized that it doesn't take 100 percent of the organization's people to change a system. After all, fewer than 3 percent of Americans fought in the Revolution. It only takes a few folks, and we were confident that there would be enough early adopters—individual who gravitate toward new approaches—to gain critical mass.

And the eighth principle was to let go of outcomes. There's some evidence that hard-and-fast objectives actually limit the possibilities.

The first year, we experimented with a number of disturbances. Although the strategy was not based on the assumption that change can only happen top down, we recognized the need to invite new ways of thinking and doing throughout the system. We were also mindful of Xerox tradition. So our initial disturbance was to offer Principle-Centered Leadership, a course derived from Stephen Covey's *Seven Habits of Highly Effective People,* to all managers. We chose this approach because it focused on the individual, it was highly personal, it helped managers learn how to create trust, and, through feedback, it allowed them to see themselves as others see them.

The workshops were organized to include cross sections of people—everyone from staff managers to general managers to first-line supervisors from all parts of the country.

Participants responded positively to Principle-Centered Leadership. Language and behavior changed. People began incorporating Covey's Seven Habits into their work. They shared the ideas with their families and colleagues. They encouraged others to participate in the workshops. The ideas, the language, and the behaviors began to unsettle the system. There was demand for increased inclusion in the workshops, and because funds were constrained, we asked that newly added participants be funded by their budget centers. People chipped in willingly for the additional sessions.

Another disturbance was a series of workshops called Leading Learning Organizations, based on the work of Peter Senge, author of *The Fifth Discipline*. Because we had limited dollars, these sessions were offered to about 120 people. I wanted to experiment with a workshop that focused on the whole interconnected system, one that took a cerebral approach to the dynamics of organizations. These sessions gave us the chance to experiment with creating shared vision, to begin ongoing conversations about the kind of community we wanted to be.

Early on, I also discovered how much learning depends on the chemistry of the participants. At the first workshop, we assembled a group of staffers who were also peers. Although there were some disagreements among the group, there was also new dialogue, deep thinking, and questioning of the status quo. It was really encouraging.

In a subsequent session, however, hierarchy reared its ugly head. Members of the senior team were included. It was a problem to blend this group with regular folks, because the seniors had strong individual agendas and didn't get along with each other. Things started going downhill when two senior "suits" had a nasty argument in front of everyone. What really iced the cake was a confrontation between Norm Rickard, the XBS president, and a workshop leader. Norm, who was Xerox's chief quality officer when we won the Baldrige Award, first got ticked off when the consultant questioned his approach to brainstorming. Then later, when she posed a hypothetical question about how executive compensation might be restructured to share the wealth more equitably, Norm about croaked. He got defensive, argumentative, and bossy and then seemed astonished when participants told him that there was a lot of fear in the organization. I love Norm, but like all of us, he has his quirks.

By this time, I recognized that in a political minefield like Xerox it is impossible to anticipate human dynamics or reactions to new ideas. But the major fallout came when seniors felt threatened. For months after the Leading Learning Organizations workshops, Norm inundated me with articles and clippings about how big weenies deserved to be paid *more* and how Ben and Jerry's couldn't find a CEO because they were capping compensation to some multiple of entry-level pay.

Another effort focused on three field operations we dubbed the Learning Centers. We selected several locations—Denver, San Antonio, and Seattle—and set out to play with new ways of working. I gathered a team of people from these sites to think and learn together, to imagine how we might change the way work gets done, and to dream up experiments.

After spending much time considering self-managed teams, we determined that XBS had way too much variation to try anything so structured. We concluded that what we wanted was a team culture, a culture of collaboration. We did come up with ways to stir up some snakes and get people thinking differently—like offering each person a free day and a hundred dollars to go out and learn anything he or she wanted: sailing, painting, crocheting—it didn't matter.

We also thought of giving every work team a thousand dollars to spend on its environments—to buy furniture or software or whatever the team wanted. As it turned out, this idea was used differently in each operation—and that was OK. Team funding was an invitational experiment.

The San Antonio operation did allocate one thousand dollars per team. Shortly after the thousand-dollar offer was published, one group announced that they needed a computer to manage customer projects. Their supervisor commented that this might be a good use of the team's money. A few weeks later, the same supervisor noticed a new computer in the account and asked if this was a work-group purchase. The account associates replied that they had convinced the customer to buy the computer. They were saving their thousand dollars for the future. I'm not sure that they ever spent their thousand dollars. They were so protective of their money that they became extremely resourceful at getting whatever they needed on the cheap. The group participated more fully in the business, increasing both revenue and profits in the process. The money was merely a symbol of their power.

As a way of introducing new thinking about work, we took people in the three operations through a two-day experience called WorkLife. In WorkLife, the participants had an opportunity to reflect on how things *could be* and how—individually and collectively—they could re-create the workplace. The experience was interesting because, again, there were no requirements for follow-up activity—no action plans, no demands, no inspection. We really left it up to the Learning Centers to decide what they wanted to try. The three locations took very different approaches and all had interesting outcomes.

The Seattle team replaced their process-management approach with one based on shared vision, trust, and cooperation. Rather than kicking back paperwork until each *i* was dotted and *t* crossed, the managers began working together to simplify the way things got done. Their collaboration paid off in real dollars. They significantly shortened the period between the time customers signed orders and the date of installation, adding incremental revenue and profits to their already fine results. Some Seattle account teams took to self-management like ducks to water. One group, based at a major Seattle law firm, turned the once shaky account into a highly satisfied customer and proposed new services that doubled the monthly billing.

The Denver operation took a fresh approach to the marketplace. Faced with competitive bidding for a large account, the general manager scheduled a meeting with the customers, talked about the kind of organization we were creating at XBS, and urged the clients to make a decision based on who they wanted as a strategic partner—not based on price. XBS got the business—a contract in excess of $1 million per month. Subsequently, the Denver operation successfully used this approach with several other customers.

San Antonio, in addition to engaging all work teams in the thousand-dollar team funding, encouraged folks to take a day off to spend a hundred dollars on learning whatever they wanted. Although the learning did not have to be work related, many people took computer classes and other courses that had direct work application.

We attempted to measure the results in the learning centers over a six-month period. We found that during our experiment, the three field locations produced $5,000 in incremental profit per person over and above the growth of other XBS field locations. Since these three locations then employed a total of about five hundred people, the $5,000 per person amounted to $2.5 million. Did this additional profit result from our experiment? Who knows? Correlation doesn't prove causality. But our hunch was that there was some connection. It is tough to apply standard mathematical models to dynamic systems. Lao Tzu compared it to "trying to understand running water by catching it in a bucket."

Concurrent with all these activities, we began a systemwide ethnographic study conducted by the Institute for Research on Learning (IRL). IRL's charter is to understand how people learn, both in the workplace and in schools. Ethnography is the approach used by anthropologists to study foreign cultures. We asked IRL to help us understand our culture—how people really learn, which systems were hurting XBS, and which were helping us. We were like fish in dirty water—but we couldn't see the water. IRL's job was to make the invisible visible. So over a fourteen-month period, we had four ethnographers hanging out within XBS—two in the field organization and two in headquarters. Talk about a commotion! Ethnographers study cultures by becoming "participant-observers," meaning that they become part of the culture yet simultaneously remain outside it.

Naturally, the XBS people were interested in the ethnographers' observations. Just their presence and the conversations that took place unsettled thinking in a big way. IRL began acquainting XBSers with new views on learning: that learning is fundamentally social, that people learn to become part of a community, that individuals who are excluded from participation in the community don't learn. Understanding IRL's perspectives on learning had an immediate effect on the way we designed learning experiences. IRL also noted "good-soldier" tendencies. Awareness of our good-soldier habits caused people to begin questioning the status quo. One person commented that IRL became a moral presence within the organization.

What had begun as an empowerment strategy had evolved into a change strategy, because the more we talked about the environment that we wanted, the more we realized that we needed to rethink everything. We had to challenge our assumptions about "the way things are" and to be open to new ways of paying people, formulating strategy, sharing information, and learning. Xerox traditionally announced new initiatives by having the head honchos "rally the troops." In other words, the company used a hierarchical communications approach. Because our strategy was to create a participatory environment that would nurture learning and innovation, we designed communications that tacitly carried messages about people, learning, and innovation. We developed a graphic theme around drawings of people representing the people of XBS. We incorporated Albert Einstein into our images because he embodied the brilliance and creativity we wanted to foster in the XBS community. By juxtaposing images of Einstein with pictures of XBS people, we provoked questioning and conversations. Good communications cause conversation, and conversations disturb the system.

With all this intense 1994 activity, it became clear that something was up. In the summer, the vice president of Marketing asked me to help design the first worldwide meeting of XBS managers. This meeting morphed into a worldwide learning conference named "X-Potential." It provided the first major commotion for 1995 and showed us the power of using large gatherings to explode new approaches exponentially throughout the organization. We designed a meeting completely outside the Xerox mold, which I'll describe in detail in a later chapter. The gathering—kind of a learning Wood-stock—mirrored the enterprise we wanted to create: a highly participatory gathering where senior managers took on support roles as opposed to leadership roles. We used music, decorations, and video to animate the gathering.

And this is how we must encourage change—by seizing opportunities to turn ordinary moments into extraordinary ones; by creating environments where people can learn together, discover together, and play together; and by doing things in a way that creates the future now. Change happens in the doing, not in the talking.

Response to X-Potential was so enthusiastic that there was an immediate demand from senior managers for an X-Potential 2 for XBS staffers. Of course, replication is a myth. As Heraclitus said, "You cannot step twice into the same river, for other waters are ever flowing on to you." So we designed X-Potential 2, incorporating ideas from the first meeting but freshening the look and shifting the content to customize the event for participants.

Over the next few months, we supported and helped design additional conferences for the finance organization, for folks in the United Kingdom, and for numerous field operations. The adoption of the X-Potential approach is a great example of the emergence that characterizes natural systems. The dictionary defines *emerge* as "to arise, to come forth, to develop, to come into existence, to come into view." So we can think of organizational emergence as the patterns that arise naturally within the community, the behaviors that develop and come into existence without direction.

Nobody announced that X-Potential was the new XBS meeting model. Rather, people recognized the power of the X-Potential design and took similar approaches for field kickoffs and other gatherings. The change strategy team supported these efforts, but XBSers took the initiative for making things happen, for disturbing the system—and they funded it, too. When people recognize organizations as natural systems and quit trying to control every variable, incredible things happen. New thinking and new ways of doing take root naturally. In an invitational atmosphere, people seize new ideas, own them, and make them better.

In the midst of supporting these large events, we decided to throw a party of our own. We had learned a lot the first year—from our own experience and from our work with IRL—and we wanted to weave this new knowledge into our disturbances. We did not have much money—especially considering the size of the organization. Plus, only three of us worked on the so-called Change Team. We had to figure out a cost-effective way to explode learning laterally through the organization. As it was clear that we couldn't do it alone; we had to find other XBSers to help. It was time to get extraordinarily creative and really radical.

I realized in 1994 that the Principle-Centered Leadership course was, in itself, hierarchical. The instructor assumed the role of the expert and, by default, put participants in the roles of nonexperts. People loved the material, and there was great demand to offer the Seven Habits to everyone within XBS. We wanted to make the Seven Habits widely available but in some fresh way—a way that reflected the culture we wanted to create. Furthermore, we wanted to introduce this new approach at a large gathering. We also hoped to introduce a game that would help everyone understand the dynamics of revenue, expense, and profit—basically Finance 101—because what we were creating was an organization of exceptional businesspeople.

Our idea was to invite people from throughout the country to an event called Camp Lur'ning. At Camp Lur'ning, we would introduce the Seven Habits, Keep the Change, and other learning experiences and encourage participants to go back, organize local camps, and spread the learning throughout the enterprise.

We invited twenty colleagues to Chicago to play with the idea of Camp Lur'ning and to experiment with prototypes of the learning experiences. Using the input from this core group, who later became camp counselors, we sent postcards to everyone in XBS, sprinkling information about this upcoming gathering into the organization. These cards were followed by invitations to nominate people—oneself or others—who loved learning, were peer leaders, and were movers and shakers—to come to camp. The criteria centered around attributes, not job experience or the candidate's spot on the organization chart.

The postcards and invitations are examples of system disturbances. First of all, the cards were beautiful and thus totally outside the Xerox tradition. The design challenged assumptions about what corporate communications look like. Second, the cards were sent directly to each XBS person—they were not filtered through the hierarchy. This was a new pattern of behavior. Third, the postcards invited a response, creating a new communication trail. The cards provoked conversations, which are how people make meaning about what is going on. Conversations often shift and expand thinking. So while we unsettled the system, we also inspired 1,500 camper nominations. And in June 1995, 220 people arrived at Camp Lur'ning in Leesburg, Virginia.

Our design approach for all large gatherings—whether it was X-Potential or Camp Lur'ning—was based on complexity theory and on how people really learn. In natural systems, information supplies the energy, the fuel that keeps the organism alive. The quickest way to generate information and energy is through chaos. We intentionally created chaos on the first day of a gathering. We observed that as people ran around trying to figure out what to do, information was exchanged, new knowledge was generated, and the gathering took on a life of its own.

In creating "white space," we gave people time and places to hang out, to self-organize. We made sure that people could choose how to spend some of their time—there were options, not rigid agendas. We remained flexible so that we could respond to things that emerged during the gathering. The participants became cocreators of the event. People got to learn in many ways and were charged to take responsibility for their own learning. Our habit of staying loose made some people very nervous—the same ones who wanted detailed, minute-to-minute agendas. We finally made T-shirts emblazoned with an "MSU" surrounded by a circle of words, "The School for Practicing Improvisation." When people asked what MSU stood for, we replied, "Making Stuff Up."

We created a rich, beautiful, engaging, fluid environment that brought out the creativity and energy in everyone. The music, food, graphics, and layout became part of the learning. We designed first and foremost for the participants. By weaving the desired outcomes—collaboration, innovation, new perspectives on learning—into what we did, we created the future now.

The first night of camp, we asked everyone to meet at the campground—an indoor area where we set up teepees; campfires; a cut, paste, and think area; a camp post office; and a camp store. It was chaotic as campers searched for their mailboxes and counselors. About ten campers were quickly tapped to organize a party scheduled for the last night of camp. There was a lot of milling around, reunions of old friends, and making new acquaintances. Titles were left at the door; people got to know each other as individuals.

The first morning, the twenty counselors, my colleagues, and I spoke about our hopes and dreams for camp. I talked briefly about the change strategy and the notion that an organization is a system that changes through disturbances. I encouraged participants to become agitators. Of course, the campers quickly latched onto the notion and dubbed themselves "raindrops" who were going to create ripples in the XBS pond.

Some campers admitted later that when they arrived, they thought we were crazy. But by the end of camp, people were bursting with energy and enthusiasm. We encouraged campers to go home and engage others in their learning. We did not ask for action plans. We provided no road maps, because XBS is such a complex environment that we knew no standardized approach would work. We did tell people how to order materials and gave them our phone numbers. Other than that, we just sent them off, hoping they would do good.

Within six months, over one thousand additional folks had taken part in camp experiences. People took highly individualized approaches—no two alike. We began sending out *Letters from Camp*, periodic mailers that described happenings in various field locations. Occasionally we would call campers to ask if they needed help. Most told us that they were getting along quite nicely, thank you very much. Although there were a few operations where not much happened, the activities that did take place created lots of buzz about camp and Partners in Lur'ning—as the camper group came to be known.

Because only a couple of senior managers participated, other seniors became curious. When we on the Change Team were asked to give presentations about camp, we instead called on campers and had them do it. A whole group came to Rochester and talked with the president and his minions. One camper flew in from the West Coast, even though his wedding was scheduled in two days. He told the seniors that although he had a lot of personal commitments, he wanted them to understand the power of camp and his belief in the approach.

The Partners in Learning loved taking on this advocacy role, and they told the story beautifully. It was another way of shifting hierarchical patterns. One camper who gave a dynamite presentation to a group of vice presidents said, "You know, we learned so much, but it never felt like we were learning so much. It just felt like we were having fun." Hot damn! What a concept! I guess fun is not the "f" word after all.

The most frequently asked question we heard in early 1996 was, "When's camp?" The expectations were high, and there was growing enthusiasm within the organization. The problem was, by then, we were operating on very skimpy funds. This is fairly predictable in an organization known for its attention deficit disorder and accustomed to the flavor of the month. There is an expectation that after a couple of years, you ought to be done.

Despite the financial limitations, we were determined to top ourselves. After playing with the numbers, we figured out that we only had enough money to fund one hundred campers. So we got on the phones, talked to our pals throughout the organization, and discovered that field operations were willing to collaborate on camp. If we would put it on, they would pay for campers to participate. They were also clear about something else: They wanted to invite customers.

The enthusiasm coming from general managers was a real high point, and here's why. Having been a general manager, I knew that GMs get paid on profit. The synonym for general manager is cheapskate. I knew that if the GMs were willing to fork over two thousand dollars per participant, then our efforts were showing up in the bottom line. Measurements in complex, dynamic systems are dicey. But when general managers pony up money, it is because they are confident that they are investing in future success.

Camp Lur'ning '96 was bigger and better. A total of 375 people participated in three days of jam-packed learning. Alumni from Camp '95 vied for thirty-five counselor spots and arrived several days early to help set up the facility, assemble materials, and decorate the place. The first evening was intentionally chaotic. With 375 campers trying to find their mailboxes and counselors and dragging customers around to familiarize them with the setup, things were wild. But, as usual, people self-organized and quickly figured out what to do. You might think that as planners we would be nervous, intervening to lessen the momentary confusion. On the contrary, we drank beer and watched things unfold. We had created the environment; we trusted that everything would be fine.

In 1996 we introduced several new learning experiences, beginning the first morning with Sleuth. Sleuth, based on the detective Sherlock Holmes, encouraged the participants to become "consulting detectives," to learn more about customers than they knew about themselves. People were divided into thirty-eight teams, each with an assigned customer. They were charged with spending the week sleuthing out information about the customer and presenting their findings on the last afternoon of camp. We set up a large resource room with connections to the World Wide Web, business books, magazines, and all kinds of markers, flip charts, cut-paste-and-think mate-rials—whatever might be helpful in creating an imaginative presentation. And although teams had a little time on the first day to agree on sleuthing approaches, most of their work had to be sandwiched in between all the other activities—as in real life. Teams members had to self-organize; they had to coordi-nate with each other, arrange meeting times, and figure out how to get the work done. Now here was the kicker: In truth there were only three customers divided among the thirty-eight teams. It didn't take long for the teams to figure this out and to pool resources. Collaboration and cooperation became the work model—and that's what I mean about weaving out-comes into the design. It's about creating conditions and sce-narios that cause good things to happen. It is the principle we must use to design organizational environments.

Although we had reserved space and time for the presenta-tions, we gave no direction about the presentation form. We really wanted to see what people would come up with. The teams turned the presentation time into kind of a learning cir-cus. All 375 campers participated in demonstrating their cus-tomer analysis—which was an energetic combination of visuals, props, and live action—with XBSers taking on the act-ing roles.

We were astonished at the depth of analysis, the innovative marketing approaches, and the enormous creativity and en-ergy that emerged from this activity. Some of the judges, who by their own admission were command-and-control freaks, were blown away by the outcome. Everyone was a winner, be-cause each group did an outstanding job. We created an envi-ronment that was fun and nurturing and brought out the best in people. Competition is about dominance and submission. That wasn't what we wanted. We went for win-win.

No matter how late I walked around the facility, there were groups of people gathered talking, looking for information on the Web, meeting about their sleuthing progress, or comparing notes about presentations. About midnight one evening, I came upon a bunch of folks sprawled on the floor creating a large banner for their customer presentation. Right in the middle of things was one of the general managers—someone with a reputation as a fashion plate. Her hair was a mess, she was in old jeans, and she was having a ball. Another member of her team later commented, "I had no idea that Liz was a general manager until after camp. That's what was so cool about camp. We got to know each other as people."

Once more, campers went back to their operations full of enthusiasm and scheduled field camps. Additionally, they began to turn other activities into camplike experiences. In some locations, "camp" became a verb. When people received some hum-drum headquarters program with instructions to "roll it out"—another mechanistic notion—they would "camp it," taking the training and turning it into something experiential and fun.

In the fall of 1996 I was invited to a local camp. The official reason for my invitation was that customers were participating and the organizers wanted me to meet them; the real reason, I think, was that this group wanted me to see what they were doing. At this location not much had happened in 1995, so I was interested to understand the approach they were taking.

When I arrived, twenty campers were sitting in a circle on the conference room floor, reading a storybook we had written, *An Absolutely Perfect Day.* I stood at the back of the room till they finished and, at the first break, visited with the campers and other people from the operation.

The GM, an old buddy of mine whom I knew to be a traditionalist, came up and said, "I bet you thought you would

never see the day that I would get enthusiastic about camp."
My friend recounted the difference that camp was making in
the environment and to the bottom line. He was amazed at
the ideas coming from former campers—ways to increase revenue, cut costs, and enhance client service. He planned to
have monthly camps so that every person in his operation
could participate along with customers.

Although there were many other activities in 1995 and
1996, X-Potential, the X-Potential spin-offs, and the two
Camp Lur'ning events caused the biggest ruckus because they
created new behavior patterns. Furthermore, there were multiple ways for disturbances to ripple out of these gatherings.

We discovered how to shift the organizational environment
by designing metaphorically dense microcosms of the enterprise we wanted, bringing people in to experience the new
workplace, and letting them decide how to re-create that back
home. We went from imagining the organization as a hierarchical up-and-down structure to thinking about it sideways, as
an organism laced with many paths that information could
travel across. The laterally moving learning experiences and
work tools were additional new ways of doing things, ones
that upset traditional hierarchical training patterns. The
events, the learning experiences, the communications, and the
artifacts generated by these new approaches unsettled the system. Because we didn't try to control what happened, we
made space for innovation and creativity. Highly controlled
environments will never bring forth innovation and creativity.
We can only get innovation by creating rich environments
where people can learn, grow, and flourish.

When individuals see new approaches, they either appropriate them or they don't. At XBS, lots of people seized these new
ways of doing things, disturbing the system as they went and
shifting the energy and work practice within the enterprise.

Since I left Xerox in 1997, there have been many changes, including shifts in leadership. Some of the new seniors were shocked at the things we were doing and have tried to revert to an old command-and-control model. From what I hear, however, commotion is alive and well at XBS—especially in the field organization—and that's because our efforts didn't focus exclusively on managers. XBS changed at a grassroots level and, like it or not, things will never be the same.

3

We Know What the Problems Are; Let's Cut to the Chase

For every problem there is one solution which is simple, neat and wrong.

H. L. Mencken

A friend in a global corporation tells about serving on a team chartered to restructure their organization. The team was headed by a real technocrat, the organization's Quality weenie, who reported directly to the president. Now, this guy loved to grill others about their "data," the processes they were using to determine solutions, and how they were going to measure their efforts. His presence sometimes prompted an exchange of the old Monty Python line: "You never know when to expect the Spanish Inquisition!" So it was pretty funny when, on the second day of the first meeting, without any data, surveys, or fact finding, the Quality guy began drawing his version of the new organization chart. First he drew a box for the president, and then—Surprise! Surprise!—he drew a box for himself. So much for data.

Several team members lobbied to spend time researching organizational design theory, but they were ignored. The group, egged on by the leader, plowed ahead with little data but lots of opinions. Oh, there was a survey. But these people could only ask what they knew to ask. And since none of them knew squat about organization design, their questions were superficial at best. When you ask superficial questions, you get superficial answers. Questions asked out of current organizational frames get answers out of current organizational frames. Not that it mattered. The new organizational charts were drawn before the survey results were in anyway. The survey was used to justify actions after the fact.

The team completed a reorganization that upset the lives of a lot of people, eliminated jobs, and led to the demotions and reductions in pay for a large staff group—and the whole thing was based on untested beliefs, shaky methodology, and a pile of questionable data. The team members were hardworking, well-intentioned individuals who got caught up in all-hat-and-no-cattle thinking. Few felt good about the effort, especially when the organization was restructured again just six months later.

The case is classic. Corporate America holds a huge bias for action over thought. Some businesspeople believe that if they do enough fast enough, they can outpace their problems. Our people say communication is an issue? Send out more and more memos. Gross margins are down? Ask for detailed lists of all expenses—including how many pencils were purchased last month. Sales are off? Let's have a promotion, cut our prices, and pound on customers to buy before year's end. All hat and no cattle. We are addicted to quick fixes that give the appearance that something is being done. Our superficial thinking leads to superficial fixes that amplify our problems. This behavior pattern can only be characterized as a headlong rush to failure.

In 1993, when I took on the challenge of designing a change strategy for XBS, I had absolutely no idea what to do. And although I visited a number of Fortune 50 organizations to understand their approaches to creating participatory enterprises, I discovered that most had traditional, hierarchical strategies. I was now reporting to the vice president of Quality, John Cooney, and I made a deal with him. If he would give me some time and some room, I would guarantee him a substantive approach. Otherwise, he needed to find someone else because I didn't plan to be part of a B movie. John agreed to fend off the president, Norm Rickard, while I figured out a strategy.

John was in an interesting position. On the one hand, he was managing a Quality organization steeped in the dogmatic, linear methodology of scientific management. On the other hand, he had me, who wanted to begin with a clean slate, to question every assumption we'd ever had about "the way things are." His was not an easy job.

One thing I was sure of. The issues that plagued us, that caused the same problems to resurface again and again, couldn't be addressed unless we looked at ourselves in a whole new way. If you want to do something fundamentally fresh and profoundly different, you approach it using methods that are fresh and different. I talked to some consulting firms. The minute they mentioned surveying or focus groups as their way of understanding the current state of affairs, I moved on. I know that surveys are sometimes useful, but having seen lots of bad ones, I love the S. J. Perelman quote: "There is nothing like a good, painstaking survey full of decimal points and guarded generalizations to put a glaze like a Sung vase on your eyeballs."

Then I heard about the ethnographic work being done by the Institute for Research on Learning in Menlo Park, California. Their field academics actually move into the study environments to become part of the culture and to experience the temporal rhythms of the place. They observe daily life, practices, rituals, and behaviors; map the patterns; and use these patterns to gain insight about the community.

My instinct told me I was onto something, so I flew to California and spent a few days at IRL and the Xerox Palo Alto Research Center (PARC). The trip was a real awakening because these places were 2,500 miles and a million light-years from the corporate culture I was used to. When I first met the legendary John Seely Brown, who heads up the Xerox research center, he kicked off his Birkenstocks and propped his bare feet on a table while we talked. It was a departure, all right.

The ethnographic teams at IRL are made up of people from many disciplines, including anthropology, economics, psychology, and sociology. I spent some time with these folks and found them extremely academic but fascinating. We began to talk about how we might conduct a broad systemic assessment at XBS. I wanted to focus on three principal areas: how people really learn in an organization, which systems were hurting us and which were helping us, and how communication really takes place.

The metaphor I often use for organizations is a fish tank. The people are the fish swimming in the water of the system. And the fish can't see the water. I wanted IRL to help us see the water—the stuff we just accepted as "the way things are"—so that we could clean it up.

At that point IRL had not conducted an assessment of this breadth and depth. In fact, to this day, I have not heard of another ethnographic study of this scope. Intuitively I thought this approach would come closest to helping us understand the deep structures and mental models of the organization; I was not sure how to convince the senior managers to do something so far out of the Xerox box. IRL had several meetings with the whole senior team, and I spent time with individual members acquainting them with the benefits of ethnography over other methods. Ultimately, they too acted largely on intuition—because they also had a real sense that we were just skimming the surface with tired old surveys, roundtables, and focus groups. They were ready to go deeper. They deserve a lot of credit for agreeing to something so different from the Xerox norm.

We spent two months on what we called Phase Zero, figuring out the logistics of the study. At that time, there were major issues between the XBS field organization and the headquarters staff. So, as part of the study, we wanted to understand this interface.

Ultimately, we placed one ethnographic team in the field. Over the course of the study, they spent time in Denver, Seattle, and Boston. They participated in all aspects of daily life, sat in on management gatherings and team meetings, worked at customer sites, and immersed themselves in the business. A second team of ethnographers studied headquarters for almost a year. I wasn't concerned about the field ethnographers' being integrated into the workplace. XBS field people are naturally open and not overly concerned with politics. Headquarters—being far more political and territorial—was a different matter. We handpicked ethnographers who we thought could handle the environment. One of them, Meredith Aronson, seemed particularly appropriate because, in addition to being very confident and self-assured, she was really tall. She could look the six-foot good ol' boys straight in the eye. What I didn't know was that Meredith drove a psychedelic car. Her old station wagon, painted in every color of the rainbow, was quite noticeable parked among the BMWs and Grand Cherokees. That was a disturbance in itself.

Over a fourteen-month period, IRL had weekly telephone conferences and periodic workshops to review thousands of pages of field notes. I spent a couple of hours every Sunday talking with Gitti Jordan, the project leader, about findings, logistics, and other issues. We were feeling our way throughout the entire project. The problem was not a lack of data or observations; the problem was how to develop themes and insightful feedback that would be helpful to XBSers.

From the get-go, we were very clear that the study would provide ideas but that it would not be prescriptive. The final IRL findings were to offer fresh perspectives on how to think about XBS issues. This was a big departure for Xerox folks, who are prone to cut to the chase. The ongoing whine to IRL was, "Can't you just tell us what to do?"

The final IRL report, *Reflections on a Journey of Transformation,* looked at XBS through five lenses: the importance of social structures to work life; the issues surrounding communication; the criticality of environments that nurture learning; the design and implementation of processes, training, and marketing programs; and the implications of rapid growth.

Social structures are elements that most of us take for granted. These structures refer not only to formal organizational entities—hierarchy, functional groups, geography, and staff/line divisions—but also to the less obvious social groupings based on friendship, shared history, special proficiencies, hobbies, and so forth.

The less obvious social groupings are known as "communities of practice" and affect organizations in surprising ways. First, communities of practice are where the latest gossip and information get exchanged and, as Robin Dunbar notes in *Grooming, Gossip, and the Evolution of Language,* "it's the tittle-tattle of life that makes the world go round, not the pearls of wisdom that fall from the lips of the Aristotles and the Einsteins. We are social beings, and our world—no less than that of the monkeys and apes—is cocooned in the interests and minutiae of everyday social life."

At XBS, communities included groups of smokers who gathered outside in the snow and rain to feed their habit, a gang of old-time XBSers who worked underground to get things done in spite of the ever-growing bureaucracy, and another gaggle of folks who played the lottery together. Communities of practice are unofficial and largely invisible but inform how we act, how we think, and what we do. We became aware of just how much of the real work gets done through these communities and the vital role they play in communication and learning. In bureaucracies, most innovative ideas are born within communities of practice—far outside the formal structure.

The concept of communities of practice is sometimes dangerous—especially in organizations hot for the latest management fad. The term quickly turned up in the XBS strategy contract—as in, "We are going to form communities of practice." Here's the deal: If you form them, then they are not communities of practice.

On the Change Team, we were mindful of communities of practice as we disturbed the system with various communication pieces and learning experiences. We noticed that within the Partners in Lur'ning, certain communities of practice emerged. We nurtured and encouraged these informal relationships in the way we organized camp—by giving people time and places to hang out. Partners in Lur'ning was really just a web of relationships within a large, bureaucratic structure.

As for communication, IRL pointed out how dependent XBS was on two modes of communication: the cascade and the "suck-up." Cascading, the traditional Xerox communication approach, is analogous to the trickle-down theory of economics, and it works about as well. Managers are sent information that they are supposed to share with their direct reports, who are supposed to share it with their subordinates, and so on. Cascading is a bit like the kids' game "gossip," in which a secret message is whispered, kid to kid, around a circle. Inevitably, when the last person shares the secret with the group, it is garbled nonsense. That's exactly how it works in organizations.

"Suck-up" communication refers to the endless staff requests for information from the field. Each staff person sees his or her request as merely a slight inconvenience, never taking into account that each demand is just one of hundreds. What IRL didn't point out and maybe didn't realize was how embedded this viewpoint is in the bureaucratic mind. True technocrats are essentially amoral—they just care about completing their task and rarely give a thought to the human implications.

XBS people immediately recognized the overuse of cascading, and lots of folks began seeking alternative communication methods. "Suck-up" continues unabated.

IRL's insights about learning probably had the biggest impact on the organization. One change took place within XBS's training organization. Everyone knew that XBS training was lackluster. And the new training director was determined to improve things. She quickly incorporated many IRL findings into Foundation Learning, a series of field-based experiences offered to all new XBSers. Foundation Learning was basically a ninety-day introduction to the business and incorporated, among other things, the Camp Lur'ning offerings. The training organization took many learning experiences from throughout XBS, wove them into an integrated whole, mapped a suggested course, and made the materials easily accessible to the field.

IRL also made us aware of two major flaws in the way we designed new programs: First, XBS constantly failed to genuinely involve users in all stages of design and implementation. Second, we treated implementation as an afterthought. Normally, we would spend a bunch of money designing something, and then—because we were out of dough—we'd just throw it out into the field and wonder why it didn't work. Several staff teams immediately glommed on to these insights, incorporated IRL findings into their approaches, and launched remarkably successful programs.

IRL's observations about XBS's rapid growth, though not surprising to field people, gave staffers a dose of reality. Because the XBS staff was increasingly made up of migrants from other Xerox divisions who had limited understanding of the outsourcing business, headquarters expectations were frequently unrealistic. IRL described field realities in enough detail that even the thickest technocrat could feel the pain—at least for a brief moment. Simultaneous corporate cries for revenue growth coupled with demands for reduced head count left XBSers between a rock and a hard place. The sticky wicket was that while the seniors were beating on field managers to cut the head count, they were hiring staff weenies to beat the band. Some seniors reacted to IRL's information in a typical technocratic way—they blamed the messenger, whining that IRL didn't tell them what to do. I wanted to say, "Don't cry down my back, baby, you might rust my spurs."

Some new folks coming to XBS were intrigued by the IRL data. One new recruit said that she joined XBS because of our fresh approaches to understanding the business. She particularly liked the ethnographic study because it provided a shortcut to sorting out environmental issues.

On the other hand, some people did nothing with the material and continued to complain about not having concrete an-

swers. They did not understand that the IRL study was designed to provoke questions. What organizations need are
communities of inquirers, people who through deep wondering and deep dialogue explore the organizational territory together.

One of the best outcomes of the ethnographic study was
that it surfaced the incredible complexity of the XBS organization—the many dynamics at play, including growth, technology, the implications of global expansion, the messiness of a
labor-intensive business, and the legacy of old thinking. The
study validated Oscar Wilde's comment that "the truth is seldom pure and rarely simple."

Because I was in ongoing conversation with the ethnographers, the Change Team continually integrated IRL thinking
and perspectives into our approach. Ethnographic insights
were particularly evident in the design of X-Potential and
Camp Lur'ning, where we created environments that nurtured
learning and communication. The camp learning products
were designed to create space for people to learn from each
other—with everyone being simultaneously a teacher and a
learner.

For me, one of the most useful take-aways was the power of
the participant-observer technique—a habit fairly easy to
adopt. We can all study our workplaces and understand them
much better by becoming participant-observers. You do this by
removing yourself from the content of what is going on and
by paying attention to the form.

When you are stuck in that next boring meeting, the
participant-observer technique can save your life. Instead of
making grocery lists or doodling madly on reams of paper, begin to notice the dynamics of what is happening. Watch people's body language. Watch who talks and who doesn't. Watch

where people sit. Watch who defers to whom. Listen to the subtext: What is the message beneath the words? Listen to the language and metaphors used. Record your observations. Share your insights with others and get their feedback. Encourage your buddies to become participant-observers too. Form a group and share your findings with each other. Be aware of your own biases and how they color the way you see and interpret your world.

Ethnography isn't the only fresh approach to understanding organizations more deeply. Another method that offers enormous potential is the Zaltman Metaphor Elicitation Technique (ZMET) developed by Gerald Zaltman, a professor at the Harvard Business School. So far ZMET has been used mostly in marketing studies for Fortune 500 companies, but based on conversations with Zaltman and his colleagues and a visit to his research lab, I believe that this approach will become a powerful tool in understanding institutional beliefs.

Through working with a representative number of individuals from an organization or identified customer group, the Zaltman method explores people's thoughts, feelings, behaviors, and attitudes about a particular topic through use of pictures, images, and storytelling. The technique brings to light the metaphors, themes, and mental models that contribute to the participants' thinking and behavior. In the course of one-on-one interviews averaging two hours, new ideas and themes emerge. Ultimately, the participants' ideas are captured in video and digital form.

Unlike surveys and focus groups, which are constrained by the very questions posed, the Zaltman technique offers participants a way to explore, to deepen, and to enrich their own thinking as part of the research process. Whereas traditional techniques focus on words, this approach taps into the nonverbal aspects of communication. The Zaltman technique recognizes that metaphors offer insights into latent ideas and needs, that sensory metaphors are as important as visual and verbal metaphors, and that lots of what people think, know, and do comes out when they tell stories.

Human thought appears to be based on metaphors, and to some extent, metaphors are shared within communities and cultures. So attention to metaphors is one way to understand the deep mental models of an organization. And since our mental models give rise to what we do, this kind of exploration can provide real breakthrough thinking.

To understand the metaphors prevalent in your community, you could engage Zaltman or his colleague Colleen Burke to do an analysis. Another way is to pay attention to common metaphors in your own environment. What do popular organizational metaphors show about the assumptions and beliefs of the community? A character in Jean Girauduox's *Madwoman of Chaillot* revealed his beliefs about people: "I tell you, sir, the only safeguard of order and discipline in the modern world is a standardized worker with interchangeable parts. That would solve the entire problem of management."

Another method for getting to the bottom of what is happening in organizations is systems thinking. Systems thinking, highlighted *The Fifth Discipline* by Peter Senge, emerged out of cybernetics and engineering theory. It is a way of looking at the interrelationships and patterns within systems—school systems, corporations, political systems, even ecological systems. Systems thinking is circular and expansive, so it comes closer to reflecting the way organizations really look.

The problem with most quality processes and tools is that they are overly linear, focus on identifying a single "root cause," and don't incorporate feedback loops. Linear processes often lead to finger-pointing, and our problems lie in the systems, not on the desks of particular individuals. Linearity has its place, but it does not always help us understand large, complex systems. It sometimes obscures even relatively minor issues. Jim Marsh of Stanford University says, "We are trying to use static models to look at dynamic issues, linear models to analyze a nonlinear world."

Living systems aren't linear; they are loopy. Living systems are open, so new information and feedback come in continually. If you are looking for root causes, you must look at organizational mental models and the structures created by the thinking. And it sometimes isn't easy to identify mental models when you are one of the people living inside the system. It is that old fishbowl dilemma again—the fish can't see the water they are swimming in.

The only way to figure out the organizational mental models is to look at the patterns of behavior. As a staffer, I became aware that the speeches, books, letters, and presentations attributed to senior managers are usually crafted by someone else. It was common to write "elevator speeches" for corporate execs, to supply them with words to describe current business strategies. This pattern perpetuates all hat and no cattle within organizations. It sends the following messages: "I'm the star, make me look smart"; "I'm too busy, too important, or too stupid to think"; "I'll use you, your words, and your ideas to get ahead"; "I'm the queen, you're the drone!" This pattern actually distances senior people from the realities of everyday life. It creates glib corporate execs with a mile-wide and inch-deep mentality. The quick fix, which has both ethical and operational implications for organizational communities, is the type of behavior pattern that would lend itself to systems thinking analysis.

Systems thinking is a way of understanding what Senge calls the "dynamic complexity" of organizations, namely, those conflicting demands—like how to grow the market, cut costs, amaze customers, increase quality, and improve employee satisfaction all at the same time. Many of us have gotten marching orders to accomplish this seemingly impossible combo. These are the times that try men's souls—and women's too.

Organizational systems are so complicated that it is tempting to throw up your hands and crawl back into your foxhole. Except, of course, that solves nothing. And because all of us create and perpetuate our workplaces, we need to become good systems thinkers—and that's not difficult. In fact, we all do it all the time in our personal lives. If you don't believe me, think back to the last time you hosted a large family gathering, the way you stewed about how to make everybody happy and keep old family feuds from erupting for three whole days. Now, that's systems thinking.

Archetypes are patterns of behavior so common—they turn up often in diverse situations and all kinds of environments—that they are named. We all use archetypes every day. When we describe someone as a Peter Pan, a dumb blond, a used-car salesman, or a lone ranger, we are using shorthand to describe a pattern of behavior.

One common archetype, "shifting the burden," refers to the organizational habit of solving a problem by applying a symptomatic solution—one that diverts attention away from the more fundamental solutions. The constant reorganization efforts prevalent in corporate America reek of shifting the burden. In a recent Dilbert cartoon, a manager proposed reorganization because "that's all we know how to do." Reorganization creates lots of busywork, meetings, and activities; it gives the impression that we know what the issues are and that we have them under control. In our busyness, we can ignore the fact that our understanding of organizations is fundamentally flawed.

Another pervasive archetype is "fixes that fail." This is the habit of reaching for quick fixes that temporarily alleviate an issue but lead to unintended consequences that, over time, make things worse. Corporate types have a knee-jerk reaction to eroding profit margins: layoffs. In this mental model, people equal expense. Unfortunately, as some enterprises have learned, layoffs may briefly improve bottom-line results, but ultimately, the diminished customer satisfaction, deteriorating workplace morale, and increased contract labor costs actually make things worse than ever. Up-front consideration of these possibilities may lead to more fundamental solutions and help avoid the pain of layoffs.

The next time you are dealing with an organizational issue—large or small—gather a group of colleagues and experiment with systems thinking. It is not important to arrive at the "right" answer. Nor is it important to draw a pretty chart. What *is* important are the conversations. That's why it is so much fun to do this in large groups and to work with systems thinking over an extended period. Through conversations, the group begins to deepen its understanding of the system and to generate a new organizational knowledge

Systems thinking is a great way to figure out issues in the moment. For example, in one period at XBS headquarters, twenty-two quality-improvement teams were working on projects simultaneously. There were lots of overlaps in their charters and in their memberships. Some people were on six or seven teams. Nobody could get a damn thing done. In a conversation with a veep who managed a big percentage of the headquarters population, we talked through the patterns that were creating so many teams. We discovered that when senior managers visited with the field, they heard lots of complaints about the unresponsiveness of headquarters. Because the seniors sincerely wanted to make things better, they rushed back to Rochester and chartered a team to solve the problems. Then, of course, because the appointed staffers were spending their lives in meetings, responsiveness to the field actually got worse. Consequently, the next time a senior was in the field, there was even more noise about unresponsiveness. So—guess what—the manager rushed back to headquarters and chartered another team, making the situation worse than before. This is a classic reinforcing loop. Once we looked at the pattern on paper, the lunacy of the situation became clear.

Systems thinking helped us make the behaviors visible. The veep participated in the conversation and, rather than its being some onerous task, we had fun playing with the loops and talking about what was happening. And it took about thirty minutes. This was not my problem to solve; I just wanted to help clarify the issue. Once this person recognized the pattern, she took responsibility for fixing it.

I've used systems thinking with groups of two hundred novices—and with that many people, you need at least twenty flip charts and a whole bunch of yellow stickies. Sometimes groups work on a shared issue; sometimes they work on problems particular to their breakout groups. It is pretty incredible to see the energy explode during these sessions. Practicing systems thinking in a safe environment—where there is no evaluation or criticism—gives rise to the very best kind of learning, the kind where people learn together through exploration and play. People discover that systems thinking is easy and fun, that it is not about answers, but about questions, conversations, and deepened understanding. Systems thinking creates in the here and now the world we are striving for—a community of learners and inquirers. After people get comfortable with systems thinking—and it shouldn't take long—it is time to take a shot at naming the mental models that lead to the patterns. Again, the answers are less important than the conversations. The awareness that our thinking leads to our actions and the subsequent search for these thinking patterns is a beginning. Systems thinking is a whole new habit, one well worth cultivating.

The reason I am so passionate about finding new approaches to understanding organizations is that I have seen the buckets of money thrown away from lack of understanding. One large global corporation recently wrote off $150 million over a two-year period on information technology projects. The corporation spent $150 million for nothing, zip, nada, bupkus. Naturally, there was lots of finger-pointing. But it wasn't a question of blame; it was a question of analyzing the system— the work processes, the culture, the mental models—to comprehend why things went awry. As far as I know, nobody in the company has done an analysis that might help people learn from this failure. Everyone's too busy running around doing stuff and, undoubtedly, pouring more money down another rat hole. Too bad the $150 million didn't buy some learning. Concurrent with this $150 million fiasco, the company was laying people off to save money.

Sometimes slower is faster. Sometimes, in our haste to fix problems, we make things worse. In our rush for cures, we end up bandaging a minor scratch when the patient is bleeding to death. To create new enterprises, new institutions, new schools, it's vital that we use fresh approaches to deepening our understanding of complex, adaptive systems. As Jennifer James said, "We move ahead by going deeper."

4

Tell Them and They Will Know

Telling ain't teaching and listening ain't learning.

Bob Barkley

Think about when you bought your VCR. Did you go home and read the instructions before you took it out of the box? Did you call a techie friend to come over and help you set it up? Or did you just plug it in and start punching all the buttons? Most of us plugged in our VCRs and just started punching buttons because lots of us learn by doing. Very few people actually read instructions.

According to validation data gathered for one learning styles profile, 21 percent of us are action learners who learn by doing, trying new things, and finding application. Another 23 percent are people learners who learn through social interaction, the experience of others, and modeling behaviors; 17 percent are a combination of people learners and action learners. People who learn purely through information—by observing, analyzing, and thinking—make up just 15 percent of the U.S. adult population. These statistics hold true regardless of age, gender, or ethnicity.

When I first saw these numbers, I had a giant "Aha!" No
wonder all the sales reps rushed to the bar after a day of Xerox
training. Most sales reps are action or people learners. And
most Xerox training is designed for information learners. Then
I wondered who learns from PowerPoint slide presentations.
The answer is NOBODY!

According to *Training Magazine,* U.S. corporations spent $58
billion on training in 1997. It's anyone's guess how many of
those dollars were wasted. My hunch is that folks would have
learned more if the organizations had built bonfires with the
money and had wienie roasts. Go into corporate training sessions and large meetings and watch how much time is spent
with presenters reading from overhead transparencies. It's lunacy!

If you look at the behaviors, you can only conclude that the
organizational mental model about training is *Tell them and
they will know.* Belief in the *tell-them-and-they-will-know* approach is so strong that even when offered facts, many corporate twits just can't accept that their presentations aren't the
greatest things since sliced bread. I'm not knocking the presentation skills of corporate managers. Gracious, they *ought* to
have good skills since this is one of the big criteria for getting
ahead. It isn't about presentation skills. It is about how people
learn. So, if learning is your goal, presentations aren't your
best bet. If performing is your goal, then by all means have a
go at a presentation; PowerPoint presentations are for the presenters—not for the learners.

There is some deep belief that knowledge is a substance that
can be packaged and placed in people's heads. It ain't. Knowledge is not a substance. Knowledge management is an oxy-
moron. Knowledge can be created. Knowledge can be nurtured.
Knowledge can be cultivated. But managed? Not likely.

Despite all the talk about learning organizations, little attention has been paid to the way humans learn. Think of the
waste—not just the waste of dollars, but the waste of time
and, even worse, of human potential. One way to get the innovation and creativity that institutions say they want is to
create environments where people can really learn and inno-
vate. Learning isn't something that happens when people go
away to take a class; it is happening all the time. And people
are either learning things that support the strategic intent
of the organization, or they are learning how to retire on
the job. IRL points out that people and communities are always learning but not necessarily what you want them to
learn.

When we are talking about how individuals learn, we need
to understand that learning happens in many ways. People
who can hear a song once and remember all the words are
probably pretty good auditory learners. These people may
think in words and may have conversations with themselves.

People who can't remember names unless they see them
written and who draw pictures to explain ideas are probably
more visual in orientation. When remembering the past, visual folks may describe an entire scene or what people were
wearing in great detail. They think in pictures.

People who remember the past by recalling how it felt or
what they did probably have a kinesthetic orientation. These
folks learn by thinking about how to make something happen,
how it will apply in real life.

Of course, thought processes are complex and interwoven,
and we all think in many ways and in multiple combinations.
Einstein combined visual and kinesthetic thinking when,
while trying to understand the nature of light, he pictured
himself seated on a wave of light looking back at the wave be-

hind him. He pictured himself doing something, imagining how that would feel.

D. A. Kolb, a professor at the Weatherhead School of Management, developed in the 1970s a learning styles inventory that has been used widely in education and less extensively in the business world. Kolb classifies learners as convergers, divergers, assimilators, or accommodators.

Remember those stated math problems we all had back in grade school? Mrs. Brown went to the store and bought 25 pounds of cheese for 30 cents a pound. The convergers, who like to focus on specific problems, are the ones writing down all the facts: Mrs. Brown, 25 pounds of cheese, 30 cents a pound. Other people are divergers; they are wondering what Mrs. Brown is going to do with all that cheese. Divergers are imaginative and interested in humans and like to reflect on concrete experience.

Some people assimilate, analyze, and synthesize lots of information, looking at things from every angle before doing anything. Assimilators are good systems thinkers, although they tend to be less interested in people than in abstract concepts.

Other people are accommodators. Give them a little information and they are off to the races. They are more interested in doing something than in understanding the *whys*—"Let's do something, even if it's wrong." Corporate America is full of accommodators.

None of these styles are good or bad. They just are. Learning-styles inventories are methods of understanding the many ways we all learn; they are not designed to label folks or put people in buckets.

When we talk about learning, we often have a "brain" orientation. But the brain is really just a metaphor for thinking and learning—as the heart is a metaphor for loving. Learning happens throughout the mind/body system. We learn with all our senses; smell, taste, touch, sight, and hearing all enter into the equation.

One way that all people seem to learn is through stories. Humans have been telling stories since becoming verbal beings. Stories were used to pass on history, to make meaning about the universe, and to share wisdom. It is not surprising that the great religious teachers used stories to illustrate principles and ideas.

Another way that everyone learns, as Arie De Geus points out in *The Living Company,* is through discovery and play. Exploring and discovering ideas for ourselves is far more meaningful than being force-fed.

These notions are about how individuals learn. The other part of the equation concerns the social dimensions of learning, which is the focus of IRL research. IRL has developed principles that debunk old assumptions about learning. At Xerox, we came to appreciate how important it is to understand social learning when trying to create environmental systems that nurture innovation.

IRL helped us understand that people are learning all the time, even in fairly dismal environments. Learning is ubiquitous and is people's most important business; it is the way we relate to the world around us. And we are either learning things that can contribute to the success of our communities, or we are learning how to keep our heads down, maintain the status quo, and get along by going along.

People have an affinity for learning, and we are all both teachers and learners. All of us can learn from others. We make a big mistake when we assume that some people have nothing to offer in terms of knowledge—that "smarts" are only bestowed on those in certain positions in the hierarchy.

People learn more easily what contributes to community success when they feel safe enough to ask questions, disagree, and make mistakes without fear of reprisal. This means that mavericks, holistic thinkers, and others who don't fit the corporate mold must be encouraged to voice their views.

People who are excluded cannot learn. When I first became a general manager at Xerox, I was one of two women out of forty-five general managers. I had to become one of the guys, become part of the bar crowd, so that I could learn. This is not to say I didn't enjoy drinking boilermakers. It was a blast. But, often, I saw things differently yet kept quiet about my views so that I wouldn't be frozen out. Consequently, the group lost the very advantage that diversity is supposed to offer—fresh perspectives and viewpoints.

People learn to become part of something—a work group, a gang, a jazz band, a social clique. Isn't it interesting that some kids who don't learn in school are fully capable of learning all the math necessary to sell drugs. Their motivation is not about selling drugs; it is about being part of a community. We all have a longing for belonging.

Learning is not separate from work; we don't have to go away to a classroom to learn something new. In fact, people usually learn best in context—by applying new learning in the moment. That's why most of us learn how to use our VCRs by punching the buttons, not by watching someone else punch the buttons or by reading the instructions.

At the same time, in many organizations, classroom learning is seen as time away from the job, an inconvenience for everyone involved. Learning is fundamental to work—part of it—and, sometimes, taking folks out of the workplace for a few days is the most effective way to create new knowledge: by giving people time to reflect, time to interact with colleagues, time to gain fresh perspectives and new ideas. We must think of learning and work in the same way that we think about breathing: Which is more valuable, breathing in or breathing out? Obviously, you've got to have both. Learning is not an either/or proposition.

Training doesn't equal learning. One observation IRL made at Xerox was the "checklist mentality" about training. The ethnographers used the example of a work group scheduled for diversity training. The group viewed a video. Afterward, instead of engaging participants in a discussion about the video's content, the facilitator just asked everyone to sign a form certifying that they "had been trained." The opportunity for learning was in potential conversations, in the interactions among participants. Conversations are where people make meaning out of information. Although the participants signed the forms agreeing that training was completed, little learning actually took place. This was a missed opportunity. This is what IRL means when it says that learning is fundamentally social and that failure to learn is the result of exclusion from participation. That's why it's important for individuals to learn in their preferred styles at least part of the time—so that they can participate more fully.

To create communities of learners and inquirers, we need to step back and take a look at everything we do, because every moment is a learning moment. We've got to create environments that are fertile for learning, learning that enables the success and sustainability of the enterprise.

When our group designed X-Potential, Camp Lur'ning, and the WorkLife learning experiences, we were sensitive to the way that XBS folks learned. Because 85 percent of the organization's workforce were people and action learners, we created experiential activities and lots of opportunities for conversation and reflection. There were enough reading and reference materials to keep information learners stimulated as well. Sometimes we suggested several learning approaches and let participants decide how to proceed.

Because we wanted to foster a less hierarchical environment, we learned to think sideways, designing content that participants could easily share with co-workers back home. Lateral learning, as opposed to hierarchical, "expert model" training, created the future now.

We wanted a collaborative culture. So learning experiences were highly collaborative—people collaborated as part of the learning process. We did not teach "collaboration." People did it. We wanted to create an organization of exceptional businesspeople. As a result, our learning experiences were about all aspects of the business, and the way that people learned together mirrored an innovative, participative, learning organization.

We were careful to arrange tables and chairs so that the space became a metaphor for forever. I recently was invited to consult with a senior management team that was trying to work collaboratively on strategy development. When I arrived, twenty people were sitting at a U-shaped table, as if they were in a war room. While this arrangement *was* metaphoric for the current organizational relationships, that was not the outcome we hoped for. I just came to a dead stop and said, "Well, before we do anything, we've got to rearrange this room." With everyone's help, we created a physical environment that mirrored the outcome we wanted—small tables where teams could sit, converse comfortably, and work collaboratively.

Because our group recognized that all XBSers were both teachers and learners and that people learn best when they know they have to teach something, we designed games, storybooks, and simple learning experiences that could be shared peer to peer. This made learning portable and highly accessible. The approach honored the capabilities of participants and disturbed the system by providing an alternative way to spread learning and create new knowledge within XBS.

Think about all the ways that learning can be made easily available to people in your own organization. Right now, lots of people see Web-based training as the latest panacea. Unfortunately, some of the new Net training courses simply take the *tell-them-and-they-will-know* approach and put it on a screen. PowerPoint slides are no more effective on the Internet than they are in the classroom.

If you want to offer Web-based courses as one option, you must remember that most learning happens in the spaces between people, when people experiment, discover, and reflect together. A few Net-based training providers believe that online communities are the answer. I don't think there is any substitute for face-to-face time—where people can talk, make meaning, and create community knowledge. In fact recent research points out that individuals who spend a lot of time on the Internet suffer from depression because of the isolation. We are social critters, like it or not.

Tom Snyder, the brilliant creator the Comedy Channel's *Dr. Katz—Professional Therapist,* had an earlier life as an elementary school teacher and frequently developed computer simulations for his own classroom. He noticed that kids learned best when they gathered around one monitor and learned together. Although competitors were designing products using the lucrative one student/one computer model, after Snyder got into software publishing, he took a different approach. He built a business based on the philosophy of one computer per classroom. Snyder has designed huge hits based on the use of computers as a community-building experience instead of an isolating exercise. "It's criminal to call what happens on a computer interactive compared to even a conversation with a dog," he says. "The dumbest dog you ever had, I might add."

Snyder's views of technology's limitations carry weight because he is a lifelong technophile. As a kid he tinkered endlessly with gadgets—rigging mechanical relays from old dial phones to transformers of his Lionel trains just to see what happened. At fourteen he jotted down some of his ideas and mailed them to the president of IBM. Several months later he arrived home from school to find giant crates filled with tens of thousands of dollars' worth of computer equipment along with a note from IBM that read: "Think of us when you're older."

The best Web training will probably model Snyder's less-is-more approach, using software to augment live workshops, learning communities, team meetings, and other social interactions. Net-based learning is not *the* solution; it is one way to make information accessible. To be truly effective, it should be used in tandem with other approaches. Also, when designing Web-based experiences, designers still need to be mindful of learning-style preferences and create approaches that honor all styles. In fact, all the elements that factor into live workshops must be considered when a person is constructing on-line experiences. How people are engaged is critical.

So what do you do about corporate training shipped to field locations with orders that it be delivered to local employees ASAP? If you find yourself on the receiving end of one of these dismal packages, don't despair. Someone I know at a large corporation takes humdrum training programs and quickly redesigns them to be fun, meaningful, and brief.

Once, she was asked to train first-line managers on the organizational human resource policy manual, a tome of more

For the learning designer:

1. Begin by imagining the best possible outcomes of a learning experience: What will people know? What will they do differently? How do you want them to feel?
2. Think through the entire experience from the participants' point of view. Will their experience produce the outcomes you hope for?
3. Reflect on how people in your organization learn. Does your design honor diversity of learning styles? Does it mirror the preferences of people in your community? Can people learn visually, kinesthetically, and auditorily? Do people get to learn together through group activities?
4. Can people choose how they want to learn? Sometimes it's fun to group folks with a variety of learning styles and let them decide how to sally forth.
5. Are play and fun part of the package? Both Ellen J. Langer in *The Power of Mindful Learning* and Humberto Maturana in his cognition studies affirm that we learn better when we are having fun and not being evaluated.
6. Allow reflection time for ideas to percolate.
7. Let go of objectives. Sometimes when we set narrow goals for a training class, we actually limit the possibilities. Think in terms of broad outcomes.
8. Create beautiful materials with lots of white space and well-designed visuals. Bag the clip art, models, pie charts, and that other boring stuff. Remember, "the medium is the message." Beautiful materials say that you care about participants.
9. Use music to augment learning. Playing music prior to the session and during breaks adds energy, fun, and meaning.
10. Design take-aways, tools, and other artifacts that keep new information accessible back on the job. When people have to explain the origin of an artifact or the message on a T-shirt, in deepens their own understanding.
11. Think about how you want to engage participants. Engagement begins with the invitation or first communication about a session. There is a huge difference between being invited and being told that attendance is mandatory.
12. Arrange physical space to metaphorically reflect the workplace you want. Classroom style does not foster community learning. Round tables with small groups do.

than six hundred pages. The training package consisted of the usual stack of PowerPoint transparencies. This creative maverick asked the managers to organize themselves into small teams and divided the manual among them. Each team sorted through their assigned pages, placing them into two piles. Pile 1 was called "occasionally handy"; Pile 2 was called "once in a blue moon." The participants had a ball, laughing over some of the nonsensical content. After a couple of hours, the teams reviewed the "occasionally handy" procedures with each other. The reassembled procedure guide was reduced to thirty pages. Everything falling into the "once in a blue moon" category was stored safely in the round file. This was a great solution because everyone knew where to find the important stuff; the rest was filler.

Because people are learning all the time, there are countless opportunities to create learning-rich workplaces day-to-day. Staff meetings and team meetings can be more productive and richer by incorporating the ideas offered for designing learning experiences. Get your colleagues involved in deciding on meeting format. Be mindful of how folks learn. Toss out overhead slides, and figure out how to engage participants in meaningful conversations and, when possible, in doing stuff. Figure out how to make tedious meetings fun—because fun fosters learning.

Think about the way your workplace is arranged. Are there places to hang out? Because, usually, when people are hanging out, visiting with co-workers, there's learning going on. IRL has a great graphic that speaks to how learning happens in the workplace; in the picture, people are climbing over the walls of cubes to talk to each other.

Although there is still a need for quiet spaces, more square footage should be dedicated to common gathering areas. At the Palo Alto Research Center, informal areas inside and out undoubtedly contribute to the innovative environment. Herman Miller, Steelcase, and other furniture designers continually research learning in the workplace and offer their insights to clients.

Lots of institutions are absolutely sterile, as if designed for robots instead of humans. If you work in this kind of environment, encourage colleagues to decorate their work spaces. My office at Xerox was filled with toys because toys make me happy. When I feel happy, I do better work—and so do most people.

Opportunities abound for creating environments that foster learning and innovation. It is not about changing the word "training" to "learning" in all your corporate literature. And it is more than bagging hollow training approaches. It is about being mindful in everything you do, seizing opportunities to turn ordinary moments into extraordinary ones. It is about transforming stale corporate environments into learning spaces. It is believing in the capacity that humans have for imaginative breakthroughs. It is about creating communities of learners and inquirers. It is about practicing improvisation. So let's start.

I love what Mary Catherine Bateson says in *Peripheral Visions:* "Rarely is it possible to study all the instructions to a game before beginning to play, or to memorize the manual before turning on the computer. The excitement of improvisation lies not only in the risk involved, but in the new ideas, as heady as the adrenaline of performance, that seem to come from nowhere."

5

You Gotta Watch
Them Every Minute

There is an automatic assumption that negative is realistic
and positive is unrealistic. Upon inspection, this is pure
madness.

Susan Jeffers

Despite all the talk espousing that "our people are our most
important asset," the systems of organizations tell a very different story. In fact, when you see what goes on in these crazy
places, you can only conclude that the true institutional para-
digm about people is *You gotta watch them every minute*. And, of
course, the second you believe it, it becomes so.

   One of my son's friends recently took a summer job with a
national retail chain. When he interviewed, most of the questions centered on stealing: How do you feel about stealing?
Have you ever stolen anything? What would you do if you
saw a co-worker steal something? After he went to work, he
discovered that everyone was searched each day before leaving
the store. The walls were plastered with signs saying, "We
Prosecute ANY Theft over $1.00" and "Cameras in Use to Pre-
vent Theft." I asked Marc how this affected people in the

/ espousing? marry

workplace. He said, "Well, frankly, it pisses everyone off so much that they spend lots of time figuring out how to steal stuff and get away with it."

This is similar to what I observed at Xerox. When I was in the field, Xerox had an unspoken belief about sales representatives—that they were party animals and avoided working whenever possible. Lots of the sales managers' time was spent tracking sales rep activity. At times, the managers asked for minute-by-minute time accounting. So, of course, what the sales reps did was meet for happy hour about three o'clock in the afternoon (you know, you have to get there early to get the good seats) and fill out their time sheets together, howling about their creative reporting. *Not working* became a value, so much so that lots of earnest reps pretended not to work hard just so they would fit in.

So, based on our beliefs, we develop management systems to control behaviors created by our beliefs—and the systems we design intensify the very behaviors we don't want. It becomes impossible to separate the chicken poop from the chicken salad. I once asked a bean counter why we had a new and very onerous expense-reporting process. His reply: "Well, you know, some people cheat." That's the spirit! Let's punish 99 percent of the folks for what 1 percent of the population does.

The time, effort, and money spent on trying to get tighter and tighter control on folks is folly. A senior manager at a credit card company admitted to me that his organization spends millions trying to control fraud, although they would actually be a lot more profitable if they just wrote off those losses. If financial performance is the main criterion, then why do organizations make these kinds of decisions? The answer is this: When people are afraid, they do weird stuff. The gonzo journalist Hunter Thompson says, "When the going gets weird, the weird turn pro." Command-and-control systems based on fear create their own pathology.

There is deep-seated fear in institutions. People are afraid of displeasing their bosses or their boards, losing their jobs, getting bad performance reviews, not making bonuses, being excluded from the in-crowd, being denied their next raises, not conforming, not being promoted, losing face, taking risks, making unorthodox decisions, broaching fresh ideas, looking stupid, disagreeing, losing control. In fact, keeping your nose clean and not making mistakes are of utmost importance. But as a ski instructor once told me, "If you're not falling down, you're not learning a damned thing!"

One reason that the all-hat-and-no-cattle mentality takes root is because mediocrity is rewarded. People who just conform, say yes to the boss, follow the rules, don't make mistakes, and don't make waves are often the very ones who get promoted. So the tacit message becomes "Be good children. You will get stars on your report cards and go to the head of the class."

Organizational communications regularly proclaim that future success depends on innovation and learning. Well, here's the deal. We will never get the kind of innovation and learning we need as long as we have systems based on fear and control. We can get efficiency. We can make money—by working people to death, laying them off, cutting benefits, and moving operations to developing countries. But we cannot create organizations where people can learn, create, and grow.

Fear-based systems breed conformity. How better to be safe and to keep your head down than by being like everyone else. Fear kills accountability and fosters irresponsibility—"I was just following orders." You're less likely to get in trouble if you do exactly what you are told to do.

Fear-based organizations thrive on insecurity and scarcity, on the idea that there is not enough of anything to go around.

In fact, many performance appraisal systems set quotas for how many high marks a manager can hand out. And the very fact that bosses decide what kind of review to bestow sows the seeds of fear-based relationships. One large U.S. corporation not only assigns numerical values to performance reviews, but also stack-ranks employees based on their rating numbers and then publishes the stacked rankings. Don't hold your breath for any risk-taking or innovation at that place.

Because of the scarcity mentality, people compete for scraps. I once saw a group of managers spend days calculating raises. The corporate beneficence that year was a whopping 3 percent. Raises had to average 3 percent, and in this instance, the employee population was both large and poorly paid. The managers argued over fractions of percentage points. I sat down and figured how much money they were talking about. I finally commented, "You guys are arguing over who gets to buy lettuce once a month and who doesn't."

Competition gives rise to infighting, backbiting, and other discord. People spend an inordinate amount of time reading the tea leaves and playing internal politics. Some organizations resemble the court of Louis VXI, where status depended on what you got to do for the king. "Look who is carrying the king's hat! And you'll never guess who is getting to wipe the king's hiney this week."

Competition leads to stealing ideas and lying. Good ideas go begging because someone else thought of them. Competition leads to risk aversion, breeding an overreliance on the past—doing the same thing over and over again and expecting different results. A purchasing agent once told me, "I'll never get fired for making an IBM decision."

People don't learn well when they are fearful and insecure. Humberto Maturana affirms what we instinctively know, that fear kills the kind of learning that fosters creativity and growth. If you ever had a hypercritical boss, teacher, or parent, you probably remember how that felt—how the pressure of impending criticism stifled your ability to be in that open, relaxed state of mind where learning happens readily.

I am continually amazed at the level of fear I see—even among seniors. At Xerox, I once helped the president and his staff with a large meeting called to announce the latest organizational structure. This gig had been thrown together at the last minute. I was coaching the group on how to organize a gathering that would foster learning and take a less hierarchical approach than usual. We did away with the stage. We figured out an experiential way for people to learn about new organizational programs. When some veeps insisted on presenting information, we created graphics that were more attractive and more conducive to learning than the standard Xerox drivel.

We had allotted a few minutes for the president, Norm Rickard, to talk about the logic behind the latest structural changes. Norm charged in at the last minute asking, "Where's my podium?" I said, "We aren't using a podium because that puts a barrier between you and the audience." On that note, Norm's entire staff evaporated. They suddenly thought of pressing phone calls or remembered that it was time to take their medication.

I like Norm. He's a stubborn guy who is sometimes a real pain in the ass, but he and I enjoyed each other and usually got along well. I turned and said, "You know I love you, Norm, and I need to tell you something. You'll never be a great speaker, but you are a terrific storyteller. Why don't you just sit on a stool and tell stories. Bag the speech."

He was taken aback, but, understanding what we were trying to accomplish, he agreed. He perched on a barstool, told stories, and was completely engaging—and he knew it. He came over afterward and thanked me for the advice. Later a couple of his staff came up to me and said, "We can't believe what you did. We would have just given him his podium."

These folks are bright, hold big jobs, have lots of experience, and are highly paid. If they're afraid to have this kind of conversation, how is fear affecting the other things they do? I was astonished at their reaction because the conversation with Norm was a no-brainer. When you care about people, you try to help them be their best. That's how I saw it and that's how Norm took it. He wasn't angry with me. You can coach people when you love them—because the love comes through.

Fear-based systems create awful behaviors. And paybacks are a bitch. The more onerous the travel-approval process, the more people work to find ways to beat the system. The more arduous the monthly reporting processes, the more meaningless the information. The more punitive the compensation plan, the more people jack with the numbers.

Maturana tells the story of some Chilean university students who lived at a boardinghouse near their college campus. A young Asian man worked there, doing odd jobs, cleaning rooms, and serving meals. These students made this young man the butt of numerous practical jokes. They were fond of tying his shirtsleeves in knots; they filled his bed with dead mice; they did everything they could think of to make his life miserable. One day they started feeling guilty and decided to clean up their act.

They went to the young man and declared that they were giving up their old ways. He was disbelieving. He said, "You mean you won't tie my clothes in knots anymore? You won't ever hide mice in my bed?"

"No, we won't do any of that bad stuff anymore," they said.

"OK," said the young man. "Then I will never again put pee-pee in your coffee."

There is no telling how much "pee-pee" there is in the corporate coffee. People who feel shat upon often get revenge—like the retail employees who stole just to see if they could get away with it. Here's the bottom line: Fear-based systems are wasting money, and more important, they are wasting human potential.

So, what's the alternative to fear-based organizations? How about enterprises based on love? What if we assumed that most folks come to work because they want to do a good job, to contribute in a meaningful way, to learn, and to grow? Love is legitimizing; fear is delegitimizing. Maturana notes that love is "the only emotion that expands intelligent behavior."

Environments based on love nurture learning—the kind of learning that helps the business. People are learning what you want them to; they aren't learning how to tinkle in the coffee. Love-based systems are safe, and when people feel safe, they gain self-confidence, become more responsible, and accept accountability for what they do. Love-based systems set people free to figure out how best to get the work done. Love-based systems grow adults, rather than petulant children.

How would we create love-based systems? First of all, we would figure out what we want to conserve about the system we have. Perhaps that is the customer base, the marketplace, or certain things about the culture. Once we figured out what we wanted to keep, then we would begin redesigning or eliminating all systems that are inherently fear based.

The first thing we'd bag would be performance reviews as we now know them. When you ask a human resources person why the company started doing performance appraisals, you usually hear about the corporation's getting sued because it didn't have enough documentation when it fired someone. Or you hear that it is the only way people know how they are doing. It's the typical corporate rubbish. If performance reviews ever had meaning, they have mostly lost it. Managers write them in a hurry because they must do whatever busywork their boss is asking for. Feedback sessions are often postponed or cut short because of the pace of the business. It's not uncommon to get your review for the previous year in March or April of the next. By then, we're talking history. If you were a hero the previous year, you can easily be a bum by spring if your "numbers" aren't where the gods demand them to be.

An engineer who once worked for my father told about the first year that Amoco did performance reviews. He went to his appraisal meeting with Dad, who summed up the previous year with these words, "I've finished your performance review, and if I told you what I wrote, you'd like it." Dad had no time for corporate baloney.

The appraisal process is just another way of instilling fear in folks, of keeping the power structure in place. A kick-ass friend of mine recently met with her new boss. He opened the conversation by saying, "For starters, why don't you tell me what your strengths are and what your weaknesses are."

"Oh, no," she said, "I'd rather start by hearing yours."

She has learned what all change agents need to know. She recognizes that people only have power over you if you give it to them. Her reply flabbergasted this technocrat manager, leaving him speechless. Every day, in everything we do, each of us is either an agent of change or an agent of the status quo. My friend is an agent of change and will not participate in any activity that perpetuates the status quo.

If there were an absolute need for some review system, we'd ask people to review themselves after seeking input from colleagues. There are organizations doing this right now, and with good results. We did it at Xerox, inside a large bureaucratic system, and people performed brilliantly. Over twenty of us agreed on group objectives and reviewed ourselves twice a year. We talked all the time and, on any given day, I could have told you what everyone else on the team thought of me and my performance—and the same was true for other team members. We often disagreed with each other and, for the most part, differed openly. Once a year we did a very loose version of a 360-degree survey, with everyone providing feedback to everyone else in the group. Each of us wrote notes to our colleagues detailing three points: what stuff to keep doing, what to stop doing, and what to start doing. It was simple, worked well, and saved an incredible amount of time.

Simplicity is the key to processes that work. A successful service organization has people review themselves by answering five questions:

- What did you accomplish last year, and how do you know?
- What do you want to accomplish this year?
- What do you need to learn?
- What is your failure pattern—how do you get in your own way?
- What can others do to support you?

People in this enterprise answer the questions and then review their thoughts with whomever they choose—a colleague, their boss, or anyone else who they think can be helpful. What's neat about this process is that it combines the previous year's review with plans for the upcoming year. All processes— like this one—should incorporate simultaneity.

My last year at Xerox, a group of field folks, Ed Leroux (the human resources vice president) and I created a new process that combined objectives, developmental action plans, learning plans, plan-and-reviews, and appraisals into one package called "Simplify," using Thoreau's quote "Simplify, simplify, simplify" as the theme. Because I left Xerox just a few months after Simplify was initiated, I was not there to midwife this new process through the system. Simplify bumped up against the petrified thinking of the process Nazis, because it was way too humane, aesthetically pleasing, and practical. Simultaneously, one veep issued his own process that was typical Xerox dreck—ugly, labor intensive, repetitive, dehumanizing—and insisted it be used. As a result, Simplify had a short life—not because it wasn't a good idea, but because of closed minds. One would have thought that with the sponsorship of the human resources kahuna, Simplify would have had a shot. But even he couldn't keep fearful traditionalists from beating a creative idea to death. A new process like Simplify needs two or three years to permeate a system because it challenges entrenched patterns of thinking and acting. The best path for new ideas is an approach of gentle integration; those implementing it must resist the temptation to say, "That didn't work" too quickly.

Lots of technocrats have a tizzy when folks don't "follow the official process. The usual whine is "But we have got to be consistent!" Remember what Oscar Wilde said: "Consistency is the last refuge of the unimaginative."

In love-based systems, we would also trash time cards, time clocks, and all the other idiocies that create robotic environments. But what about laggards? How would we manage those perpetually late people? By exception, that's how. We wouldn't punish 99 percent of the folks in an attempt to manage the

*Aesthetic: Concerned with the study of the mind & emotions in relation to the sense of Beauty

1 percent. By the way, if you have been told that time cards are "the law," that's hogwash. They're not.

Another change we'd make would be in compensation systems. The problem with most current pay systems is that they are based on all hat and no cattle, on the notion that people are motivated by reward and recognition, by the great jackass theory of carrot and stick.

Current systems are often punitive, discriminatory, and inherently unfair. They continue to widen the gap between the haves and the have-nots. Tons of research has proved that pay does not, in itself, motivate people. There is also evidence that our obsession with pay and the unfair nature of current pay structures create so much anger and resentment that the net effect is one of de-motivation.

For most people, actual income has fallen in the past thirty years. The only exception is executive compensation, which has risen disproportionately to the rest of the population. Executive pay is obscene. I mean, these folks make feudal lords look like philanthropists. Proposed legislation to limit the amount that corporations can write off for executive perks has been defeated, thanks to corporate lobbyists. And guess who gives office holders most of their campaign money? You've got it, corporate donors.

For best results, pay needs to be made a nonissue and, to some extent, should be separated from individual performance. There is no evidence that "pay for performance" contributes positively to business results. We need to pay everyone well, based on published principles, principles agreed upon by people inside the system. All the talk about using benchmarks to set pay levels is horse pucky. Did you notice that nobody ever shows the benchmark information? Current systems are so flawed that if you ask someone to explain them, all you get is double talk and weasel words. Equitable systems would be easy to understand and open to review by everyone in the enterprise. Everyone, through profit sharing, gain sharing, and stock ownership would participate in the overall success of the business.

In love-based systems, we would create learning environments that were safe and designed foremost for the participants. We would understand that when people are hanging out in the hallways or on the production floor, there is learning going on. We would engage everyone in running the enterprise, which would mean, at the very least, educating every person in business fundamentals. We would open the financial books. We would put our money where our mouths are and invest in "our most important assets." We wouldn't cut benefits and wages of regular folks when corporate officers are raking in millions.

Productivity wouldn't be solely based on doing tasks. I recall how XBS measured productivity for printing jobs, specifying that in an 8-hour shift, people should be fully productive for 6.5 hours. When those numbers were off, I had some explaining to do. We didn't run our operation by the book, and most of the time, our results were excellent. We had creative people who worked really hard. Sure, occasionally there were screwups, but we knew that you cannot treat people like machines. You have got to leave room for innovation. And, if you're beating on folks to get robotic-like output, you're making a short-term decision. Sometimes we made short-term decisions, and every time we did, we kicked ourselves. Over time, we did best when we agreed on what needed to be accomplished and then got out of the way. That's what we would do in love-based systems: agree on what needs to be accomplished and then let people figure out how to make it happen.

Let folks expand their jobs. Design jobs so that there is room for people to stretch and grow. One vice president at Xerox had apoplexy every time he heard "get out of the way." He inferred that meant that leaders had no role—and that's not what it means at all. It means that we move from a leaders-as-managers model to a leaders-as-environmentalists model.

Even if you are inside a large bureaucracy, you can begin to create a love-based environment. My experience is that 99 percent of the time, when you trust the people you work with, they will continually exceed all expectations. People who feel good, do good. Will you sometimes be disappointed? From time to time, individuals may take advantage of you. But it is not worth worrying about. Trust people, and at the end of the day, you'll be ahead of the game. When someone violates your trust, that is about them, not about you.

A pal of mine tells the story of starting work for a new boss. "I walked into our first meeting and my heart sank when I saw my personnel file sitting on his desk. Golly, it was thick. He handed it to me and said, 'I haven't looked at this. Go through it and take out anything you want to remove and add whatever you want to add.' He earned my trust immediately because he trusted me. I worked my heart out in that job because I felt safe and free to be myself."

Whenever you're making a decision or contemplating a course of action, ask yourself, "Am I coming from a place of fear, or am I coming from a place of love? Am I trying to control things, or am I creating space where people can be their best? Am I creating a workplace where I want to spend my life energy?" Dee Hock, the founder of VISA, puts it well: "If you're a manager, think about the stuff your previous managers did that you liked and do that. Think of what they did that you didn't like and don't do that."

We create our environments and they create us. And as we change, so do our environments. Maturana, whose research confirms this dynamic, summarizes co-creation with the words of the Spanish poet Antonio Machado: "Life is a path that you beat while you walk it."

The idea of self-creating systems has long been part of the Australian Aborigines' belief system. The Aborigines say that each day, we sing our world into existence and it sings us. So maybe it's time to sing new songs.

6

Meeting Equals
Data-Dump

Real wealth is not gold.
Real wealth is knowing what to do with energy.

Buckminster Fuller

Want a perfect example of all hat and no cattle? Organizational meetings. All enterprises have meetings: sales meetings,
finance meetings, planning meetings, kickoff meetings, big
meetings, small meetings—but mostly awful meetings. Take
kickoff meetings. Or, as Henny Youngman would say, "Take
kickoff meetings, please!"

For starters, everyone gets memos about the time and place
and, as always, is reminded that attendance is mandatory. On
arrival, the participants attend a big cocktail party, where people get ditch-crawlin' drunk because they know what's coming. The first morning, the head honcho opens the festivities
mouthing the usual platitudes: how much the organization
loves its people, how important innovation is to success, how
important learning and empowerment are, blah, blah, blah.
Sometimes there is even an inspirational video "to fire 'em

up." As one of the characters in the movie *Get Shorty* said, "I've seen better film on teeth."

After that, the other seniors get up and pontificate about their functional areas. Their fawning introductions of each other are endless—what those of us who have witnessed this aplenty call the mutual masturbation portion of the program. Typical speeches include exhortations to get back to blockin' and tacklin', to beans and bullets, to readin', ritin', and 'rithmetic. Mixed metaphors are very big in this crowd.

Next comes recognition. Corporate types sounding vaguely like game-show hosts hand out some tacky plaques. Of course, just a few people are recognized, so the rest of the crowd sits there feeling like voyeurs.

Following such an opening, there is bound to be a letdown. From then on attendees are herded like cattle into a series of dark rooms to view one PowerPoint presentation after another—you know, the slides from which the presenters read verbatim? This goes on day after day, sometimes way into the evening. At the end of the ordeal, folks are given fifty-pound binders filled with copies of the slides. They lug these burdens home, plop them on bookshelves, and never look at them again.

I wish I could say that such dismal gatherings are limited to just a few organizations—or even just to the corporate United States. Unfortunately, this plague is widespread, extending to conferences that people actually pay to attend. I recently went to a meeting organized by people noted for their forward thinking. The opening speaker, the CEO of a U.S. enterprise, talked at length about his company's culture change effort. He said, among other things, that his business used to be a good ol' boys club, but that things were really different now. At the end of his talk, he invited some other people to help him field questions. Guess what: Everyone who came to the stage was a white guy! Oh, there were women from his organization present, but they were not allowed up front with the hombres.

This is a good example of what organizational theorists call the difference between the espoused theory and the theory in use. The difference is the gap between what is said and what is done. When I went to college, the espoused theory was that I was there to study. The theory in use was that I was there to party. In the CEO's case, he talked about embracing diversity and then surrounded himself with white men.

This gap between the espoused theory and the theory in use is the biggest reason that people disbelieve 99 percent of organizational propaganda. It is the reason that folks don't buy in to efforts aimed at change. The idea that people resist change is hokum. Humans are designed for change. It's the way we survive. People resist having change *done to them*. They resist efforts that cry out, "Do as I say, not as I do." They resist idiocies that will disappear shortly to be replaced by the latest flavor of the month. People resist inane organizational programs because people are smart.

Organizational meetings crystallize the gap between espoused theory and theory in use. Despite the talk about empowerment, innovation, and learning, the way these meetings happen are the very antithesis of those things. How empowering is it to be herded from one room to another with no choice in the matter? How much learning takes place with slide presentations, when few humans learn that way? Who would believe the blather about innovation when these damn meetings have looked the same for the past twenty-five years?

It doesn't have to be this way. Meetings offer huge potential for learning and for revitalizing organizations—because meetings are a microcosm of the organization—and most of us, from time to time, help organize and plan gatherings. Meetings provide a great venue for new doing. And that's where change happens: in doing things differently.

At Xerox, our team figured out how to turn big gatherings into disturbances. What we did was simple—we thought about what kind of organization we wanted and then we created it in the moment. We disturbed the hell out of the system. One reason the meetings were a hit was because we closed the gap between the espoused theory and theory in use. The gatherings rang true.

As explained in Chapter 2, our first experiment took place in January 1995. It started as a standard kickoff. The difference was that the veep responsible for this shindig was willing to try something new. After all, this was the first gathering of XBS managers from around the world, and Sharon Browne knew that if there were ever a time for a fresh approach, this was it.

Sharon and I had been pals for a while, and she liked the stuff we were doing with the change strategy. She asked me to get involved, to work with the team responsible for bringing the whole thing off. These were great people. I liked them but knew we'd face inevitable petty jealousies and old mind-sets. I jumped into the fray because this was a huge opportunity for disturbance, and disturbance is where change happens.

Petrified thinking showed up at the initial meeting when the very first agenda item was "the mission statement." I'd rather eat dirt than write another mission statement. Folks began droning the usual corporate speak—standard dreck. The energy just drained out of the room. Finally I said, "We can't start this way. If we have to do a mission statement, let's write one that is fun!" People looked hesitant. The possibility of a mission statement's being fun was a new notion. A few technocrats protested that it had to meet Xerox standards. Oh, please! We finally wrote a fun mission statement: "We are some XBS people bringing XBS folks together for the first time from around the world to learn and have fun so our customers will like us enough to buy from us over and over again."

That shifted the thinking. We began to consider how, for once, to design a gathering strictly for participants. We talked to a bunch of people in the organization and found out what kind of meeting they wanted. We knew we'd have to fight off predictable staff demands to present the latest warmed-over corporate crap. Staffers get so wrapped up in the nits that they forget that field people are interested in a couple of things— where are we going and how are we going to be successful?

The field managers we talked to confirmed our hunches. They didn't want to waste time being told stuff they could read. They wanted to talk about the future of the business, to spend time with each other, and to have some time off. They did not want a transparency parade.

Finding out what participants wanted was the easy part. The bloodbath took place over how to design the meeting. Diane Thielfoldt, one of my Change-Team colleagues also on the planning team, fought this battle with me. Diane is brilliant at working the network, at being a peacemaker, at thinking through the thousands of details that have to be taken care of. I am the opposite. I'm big picture; I know how to create what folks tacitly want, how things should taste, sound, and feel. I am interested in every detail as it contributes to the environ- ment—especially the music—but I always team up with some- one like Diane, who could organize an army. She helped me get beyond my impatience with distractions—with what I refer to as the "dragging Charlie" part of the process.

This expression comes from one of my dad's favorite jokes about the golfer whose wife asked about his Sunday game.

"Oh, it was terrible," the golfer said.

"What happened?" his wife asked.

"Well, Charlie had a heart attack and died on the first hole."

"My God, that's awful!"

"Yeah, you wouldn't believe how awful. The whole rest of the day it was hit the ball, drag Charlie, hit the ball, drag Charlie."

Well, on projects like this one, unless you are content to go along with an old, tired, stale approach, you'll spend a lot of energy "dragging Charlie." Everything we wanted to do challenged the status quo. Every detail was a battle. Diane and I threatened daily to quit after the whole thing was over. The rest of the planning team was just as frustrated, but we all plowed on despite heated disagreements.

We wanted to design the gathering so that people could really learn. After all, the change strategy was about creating an environment where learning and empowerment flourish. Our intention was to make these words reality in the design of the meeting.

Since almost nobody learns from presentations, we knew that we had to break the nasty organizational habit of reading off slides from dawn till dark. That meant, for once, we'd have to be disciplined and selective and establish criteria for who would speak. It also meant that the seniors wouldn't get to do their little dog-and-pony shows.

We were also determined to design great visuals and rehearse speakers to engage participants rather than boring them into a stupor. As the meeting time got closer, seniors began asking, "When do I present?" The answer was, "You don't. Y'all just come and have a good time."

Because we recognized that most learning happens in the spaces between people, we designed reflection groups that gathered periodically throughout the four-day event—to talk about what they were learning and about how new XBS products would play in the various marketplaces. Our plan was to create reflection spaces throughout the hotel. Staffers quickly stepped in with offers to facilitate the reflection groups. They argued that people just couldn't be turned loose with no direction. After all, how would they know what to do? Besides, if left unguarded, everyone would go play golf or goof off! There's that mental model about people—*you gotta watch them every minute.* We fought this battle until the meeting started. We finally agreed to let staffers hang around the breakout rooms in case they were needed. Of course, the groups got so engaged in conversation that they totally ignored these guys. And, guess what? People didn't goof off, and even more amazing, they knew exactly what to do. Of course, because people are smart, it's organizations that are stupid.

We also had to find a way to make lots of information available that wouldn't be included in presentations. So we created a large exposition space called Xpo, where participants could go to learn about new Xerox products and the latest corporate programs. Many of the twenty-five booths offered hands-on learning opportunities. Folks had a choice about whether to go to Xpo, how long to stay, and what to learn. Because Xpo wasn't mandatory, naysayers claimed that nobody would show up. The participants not only showed up, they wouldn't leave. We had to chase people out of the place about nine o'clock each evening so that we could go eat dinner.

The creation of the overall environment began long before the gathering. We veered 180 degrees from the usual Xerox drill, gave the meeting a cool name, and developed a distinctive graphic theme that was interwoven into the invitations, correspondence, ticket covers, luggage tags, and all other meeting materials. The name X-Potential captured the mood that we wanted—that XBSers had the potential to grow exponentially, both individually and collectively. Diane Thielfoldt, the detail goddess, was determined that for once, people would receive invitations, tickets, and materials with their names spelled right. This would appear to be no big deal, right? Wrong! XBS systems are such a mess that it was near impossible to figure out who was coming and where to send their invitations and tickets, much less how to spell their names. Diane spent hours poring over the lists. When you are creating an environment for participants, they must be cared for in every single moment. How would you feel if your name were spelled wrong on your invitation? To neglect this detail would have created one of those nasty gaps between what we espoused and what we did. Details can make you or break you.

The invitations, the name X-Potential, and our billing the gathering as a worldwide learning conference provoked lots of questions and conversations. Although initially we were counting on about 200 participants, the group swelled to 450, complicating the lives of the planning team trying to celebrate the holidays before heading to Florida. We flew south right after New Year's with an overwhelming amount of work to do before everyone arrived. For this kind of gathering, most of the effort is up front because the planners' job is to create the environment. After the meeting starts, the participants make things happen.

We planned the gathering by weaving the outcomes we hoped for into the design. The organizing team wanted participants to feel like the stars; to understand the power of collaboration and diversity; to recognize that although each person is responsible for his or her own learning, the organization must create environments that foster learning. We also wanted people to leave with tons of new ideas that would wow our customers and guarantee continued success.

When folks arrived, video crews interviewed participants from around the world. The first morning, everyone walked into a room festooned with stars and moons and filled with music. The lights dimmed, and up popped a video filled with clips and interviews from the day before. After the president made some short introductory remarks, Dee Hock, the founder of VISA, spoke about the need to create "chaordic" organizations, enterprises that toe the line between chaos and order and are run from the periphery by people closest to the business. A great speaker with a very engaging manner, Dee validated that we were on the right path. He had lots of credibility because he isn't a theorist; he is a practitioner with proven business success.

After a few other remarks from Xerox's CEO, we asked the participants to gather in their reflection groups and talk about their shared visions for XBS. This wasn't about writing vision statements; it was about conversations. Participants drew their visions in pictures; we later hung these banners throughout the facility.

The sponsoring veep was concerned about this shared visioning notion. "What if their visions aren't the same as ours?" she asked. I responded that although the visions wouldn't be identical, my bet was that they would be congruent. And, of course, they were, because most humans want the same things—a meaningful workplace where people can be happy and successful. The power of shared vision is that it's not imposed; it comes from the hearts of the folks in the organization. The strongest theme running through all these visions was that future success depends on XBS people.

The entire first day was designed to create context. It was about *being*, not about *doing*. One obvious missing element was the usual recognition. During the setup, we talked briefly about the design principles, including the fact that because everyone in the room was part of XBS's success, this wasn't the time for individual recognition. The participants cheered. We always knew that if the first day went well, we were home free. It did, and we were.

That evening we opened Xpo. The graphic themes and care for the environment were reflected again in the Xpo area. It was beautiful and designed for mingling, good conversations, and hands-on learning.

The subsequent days focused on marketing, on technological innovations that were rapidly changing customers' expectations. Each day began with a fun video featuring the participants.

Music, carefully selected, played during breaks—everything from classical to rock to songs from around the world. This added incredible energy and metaphorical diversity. We alternated presentations with reflection and hands-on time in Xpo. We had large, standing cardboard Einsteins around the meeting areas. When we needed to post breaking news or announcements, we put it in Einstein's hands. The Einsteins began disappearing on the first day and we pleaded with participants to leave them till the end of the conference. After the meeting, I spotted one European sneaking a stolen Einstein through the airport. I don't know how he got him on the plane.

We videotaped everything and made complete sets for every participant. We served cookies shaped like Einstein. Although we asked people to take responsibility for their own learning, we made sure that diverse learning styles were honored and that folks could learn with all their senses.

During the entire week, there was a total of eight hours of presentations. One staffer commented that he once would have found this ludicrous—before he understood how people really learn.

Early in the week we grabbed a group of participants to plan a big party for the last night. We had reserved the space, but this group dreamed up the theme, got the musicians, invited everyone, and made it happen. They also went out and rented a bunch of guitars, and folks from all the countries sang late into the evening. It was so much better than any party we could have planned and, of course, it modeled the richness created with participation and diversity.

X-Potential was an unqualified success; the whole planning team felt really great. The only gripes were from a few seniors who missed being front and center. We also got blamed for the meeting's going over budget. This was ridiculous, of course. It went over budget because it grew from 200 people to 450. One thing I have learned over and over is that no matter what you do, you'll have some detractors. A couple out of 450 wasn't bad.

We took the principles underlying X-Potential and used them again and again. Camp Lur'ning, described in Chapter 2, looked different from X-Potential, but the design principles were the same. They are principles that anyone can use—in large meetings or small.

- Work from big ideas. X-Potential and Camp Lur'ning are big because they are about forever. To name the gathering something like Kickoff '95 would have been a narrow notion. It wasn't about 1995. It was about the future of XBS.

- Create in the moment the world you want forever: In other words, make the future happen now. Don't talk collaboration, do it; don't talk innovation, be innovative; don't talk about empowerment, give people choices; don't talk about diversity, incorporate diversity; don't talk about flattened organizations, be one; don't talk about customer satisfaction, satisfy the partici- pants— the customers for the meeting; don't talk about learning, do it.

- Remember that you are dealing with a natural system. Don't worry about a little chaos; stay flexible so that you can shift plans when the group comes up with ideas that enhance the content or the texture of the meeting. Once people become cocreators of a gathering, they may want to move things around or spend more time on a particular activity or subject. Go with it.
- Create environments where all learners can learn.
- Create content, space, and materials that respect the participants.
- Weave outcomes into the design.
- Use music—all kinds, carefully selected.
- Use videos only if they send the right message.
- Engage participants in co-design.
- Understand that every detail sends a message.
- Make it fun!

The biggest barrier that anyone planning a large event will encounter is all hat and no cattle. Good ideas get rejected all the time, not because they aren't good, but because they chal- lenge old beliefs. New approaches are very scary for folks who have "made their bones" doing things the old way.

Recently I spoke with someone whose organization has an annual sales meeting designed on a "tell, tell, tell" model. This person commented that "we're always in a hurry, and it's just safer to do it the old way." When I asked him how much it cost to bring 150 salespeople together, he estimated $2,000 per person. I pointed out that even if they were getting half of the optimal results—a generous estimate—they were wasting $150,000. With some basic redesign, their money could be much better spent.

The next time you are involved in designing a meeting—large or small—here are some ideas to consider.

Start with the big idea. Then design a graphic theme that carries that message in words, pictures, and design. Send invitations that provoke conversations and questions. This will begin to create a buzz and maybe even the hope that something fun is on the horizon.

People will protest that you can't afford to create good materials, that they cost too much, that there is not enough time. Malarkey! The problem is not in the expense or the time; it is finding someone with enough imagination to create stuff that is aesthetically pleasing, takes a "less is more" approach, and respects the intelligence of recipients. You can create beautiful materials that can be duplicated in-house. All it takes is some well-designed originals.

Technocrats will resist giving up slide presentations. It's the old "I had to walk to school barefoot in the snow—uphill—so everyone else should too." I don't know why this is so tough for traditionalists to understand. Recently I attended a conference for managers of corporate universities. Most of them used slides that—in the words of that famous poet Bo Diddley—looked as if they'd "been whupped wid an ugly stick."

If presenters insist on slides, design engaging graphics. Don't let anyone fill slides with words that they then read verbatim. Those kinds of slides are for the presenter, not the participants. In fact, one good question to ask constantly is "Who is this for?" This keeps everyone honest.

The best way to make your argument for "new doing" is to write down all the espoused theory and then match it up to what is planned for the event. Get folks to consider the gaps you're creating if you say one thing and do another. Use research information about how people learn—sometimes that helps.

You'll probably have to find a way to remind seniors that the meeting is for the participants, not for the pooh-bahs. One very subtle way is by saying, "Oh, I was confused. I thought this meeting was for the participants. Now, I understand, it is for you!" No, on second thought, you'd better come up with something else.

When you are planning the music, don't just pick your own favorites. I've been to one public conference that has played the same music for the past five years—I assume because it's the organizer's favorite. So who is the conference for, anyway? And what kind of message does that send about diversity? If you can figure out how to do it, have the participants bring music they love, and then play that.

Scrutinize any videos for the kinds of messages they send. Most that I've seen are condescending or are so boring that they could cure insomnia. Typical videos star the seniors, not the folks. The videos we did at Xerox were short, fun, energetic, and filled with participants. The message: "You are the stars of the show!"

Arrange the physical space to reflect metaphorically the kind of organization you want. Round tables work well. Yes, they take up more space, but consider how different you feel sitting at a round table instead of sitting auditorium style or at long tables with Mom or Dad at the head.

If you have breakout groups, try to keep them to four people. Although we created groups of eight to ten, I learned later that that conversation is difficult to sustain with more than four people. The next time you are at a party, watch the dynamics. When more than four people begin to talk, the group will eventually split into smaller units.

As a rule of thumb, try to limit presentation time to a couple of hours a day. The rest of the time, participants should be engaged in doing stuff or in learning from each other. This doesn't mean sending them into breakout business meetings to get hammered on by some dweeb. What gets most groups into trouble is trying to cram too much information into too little time. When that happens, folks don't learn squat. Set up an exposition-like learning lab where people can discover things they are interested in. Don't force-feed information; it is a waste of time and depletes everyone's energy.

Get participants involved. There is no reason for the organizers to plan everything. Turn the party or parts of the agenda over to the group, and watch what happens.

Look at what messages the details send. Having participants pick up their souvenir T-shirt out of a pile on a table sends quite a different message than giving folks T-shirts that have been folded, tied with a ribbon, and placed on their pillows. Those kinds of touches show that you care.

Some people along the way will probably ask the heinous question "How are you going to measure whether this works?" If they do, ask them what "works" means and how they are measuring effectiveness now. William James aptly described the idea of trying to quantify success: "Objective evidence and certitude are doubtless very fine ideals to play with, but where on this moonlit and dream-visited planet are they found?"

So how will you know? If everyone is energized at the end of the day, that's good. If they are exhausted and make a beeline to the bar, that's not good. Design the right kind of gathering, and the energy will be tangible and will spill over into the workplace. You'll really know it was a success when everyone starts wanting your advice and copying what you do. But mostly, you'll just know.

The best feedback I got at X-Potential was from somebody brand new to the organization. In fact, her first day was the same day this happening started. She commented, "When I got here, I didn't know what to think. I'd never seen anything like it. By the second day I was praying that I never have to go back to my old organization. This is clearly the place to be."

7

Father Knows Best

> Having power means, among other things, that when
> someone says "This is how it is," it is taken as being that
> way. . . .
>   Powerlessness means that when you say, "This is how it
> is," it is not taken as being that way.
>
> **Catharine MacKinnon**

It's funny how human history manifests itself in institutional
life. Listen closely to everyday assumptions, and you will hear
echoes of Puritanism, classism, rationalism, and patriarchy.

H. L. Mencken defined Puritanism as "the haunting fear that
someone, somewhere, may be happy"—a terror obviously
shared by the technocrats who dream up all the onerous
processes and rules. And although nobody in corporations
wants to talk about class or elitism, John Malloy, author of
Dress for Success, claimed correctly that if you're not upper
middle class, you'd better look it and act it if you want to "get
ahead" in the corporate world.

Patriarchy goes hand in hand with hierarchy. Think about
how much an organizational chart looks like a family tree. Patriarchal thinking gives rise to the whole trickle-down theory
of wisdom that I call *Father knows best.*

There is some broad belief that the "suits" possess wisdom that lesser beings don't have. Sometimes seniors *do* have access to information that others don't. There are some smart folks in top jobs. But let's not confuse smarts with wisdom or judgment.

Recently, a Fortune 500 corporate veep visiting a manufacturing location was invited to make a few comments during an evening business meeting. People were exhausted. Many had been working on the production floor since early morning and were ready to call it a day. Now, you'd think that under these circumstances, the corporate twit would have had the sense to say a few well-chosen words and let everyone go home. Unfortunately he saw it as an opportunity to share his great wisdom with the common folk.

He stood before them in his Armani suit and recounted what he had done to become so successful. He described a typical day in great detail:

> I get up every morning at five A.M. so that I can exercise in my home gym for an hour because, you know, it is really important to be physically fit. Then I get to the office by seven so I can have some quiet time before my secretary arrives and the phone starts ringing. I work till seven at night, then rush home to have dinner with my family. You know, time for your family is very important. Then I work in my study till midnight. I have learned to survive on five hours' sleep, and you can too.

Unbelievably, this guy droned on for two hours using *himself* as the example of how everyone should live his or her life. He seemed to see no disjoint between his lifestyle with a home gym, a study, a secretary, and a stay-at-home wife who has dinner on the table at seven o'clock sharp each evening—and the lifestyles of his audience, who, for the most part, come from households where everyone works just to make ends meet. Nor did he have any shame at holding himself up as an icon of hope to the riffraff.

Now, this is a guy considered one of the best and brightest by the powers-that-be in his company. He's tall and good-looking, wears expensive suits, and is famous for throwing lavish kickoff meetings where he is the star of the show. His inability to tell giddy-up from sic' em doesn't seem to register with the "suits," because they, of course, want *to be* him.

Patriarchal attitudes show up all over the place—even in pretty wonderful folks. A woman I know was recently called to her boss's office to hear some "good news." This guy, who is a genuine gem of a person, announced proudly that she had been selected to be executive assistant to the company president—a job reserved for fast-trackers. The woman was flabbergasted since she loved her current assignment and the city where she was living. She couldn't believe that "the boys" had decided her future without consulting her, assuming that she would be thrilled to relocate one more time, travel extensively, and do a job that held no appeal for her. This normally cool customer let her boss know just what she thought of the decision. She ended by growling, "Find someone with a penis to take the notes!"

The problem with patriarchy is that it appears benign, even desirable, to patriarchs. I know a genuinely kind and caring guy who continually referred to his secretary as "little Ann." He was stunned when I called his habit condescending and insulting. Although he immediately quit saying "little Ann," he really couldn't grasp what I meant by patriarchal behavior, probably because it is his basic style, cultivated over many years, and it feels as comfortable to him as a pair of old shoes.

Lots of people, including some whom I respect, believe that change has to start at the top, that if the managers are not on board, nothing will happen. I challenge this notion as arising from the patriarchal attitudes buried deeply within all of us. Most change agents and consultants claim that although they start at the management level, they plan to engage everyone else eventually. Except, of course, it seldom happens. If all you do is hang around with managers, you become part of the hierarchy yourself.

Management is certainly an important part of the picture—it's just not the *whole* picture. Although managers do plenty to reinforce the hierarchical system, people within organizations also perpetuate the status quo by unnecessarily asking permission, by kowtowing to seniors, by treating managers as if they are all-knowing and all-wise, or by acting hierarchical themselves.

Someone I knew at Xerox used to talk about the top two hundred Xerox managers as if they were a heavenly group of angels and archangels. His voice would take on a tone of deep reverence, and he'd get all starry eyed. I expected him to genuflect at any minute. When I was invited to speak to this crowd, he kept dropping hints about how I should act in such august company. I finally said, "Look, there are two schools of thought. One is that these folks are special just because they happen to be in certain jobs. The other school is 'one leg at a time.' I am from the second school—so I'll act with them just as I do with everyone else." Jesus wept.

Senior managers catch a lot of criticism—and lots of it they bring on themselves. Managers get themselves into trouble when they begin to believe their own bushwa doesn't stink. That's what happened with the corporate veep who bored everyone silly for two hours describing his own perfection.

Since that evening, his comments are parodied anytime his name comes up. People say, "Oh, I must get home because my wife will have dinner on the table promptly at seven, and, you know, its really important to spend time with the family." His patriarchal and elitist behavior, not atypical among managers, unfortunately corrodes trust and reinforces hierarchy. It smacks of *Let them eat cake*.

Speaking of *let them eat cake*, several years ago, a Xerox finance dweeb sent out what we referred to as the standard "bagel and donut" memo. About twice a year, immediately following a financially bad month, some bean counter issues a memo exhorting employees to turn off the lights, to cut down on overnight mail, to use fewer pencils, and to quit ordering bagels and donuts for meetings. I am not making this up. This is the way financial wonks prove they are right on top of things. Wouldn't the stockholders be proud?

Now, usually folks respond by pitching the memo. This time, however, people were really ticked off because the very next day, fifteen senior cowboys took off to Europe for a week—and all but one flew business class. A veep named Dick Kievit realized that there was a problem—the behavior wasn't matching the words—and although he screamed and hollered, his protests fell on deaf ears. He then did what *he personally* could do. Although he had to go to the meeting, he traveled economy class. That's why everyone loves this guy. He has integrity. His walk matches his talk.

Let-them-eat-cake behaviors are not confined to corporations; they are painfully apparent in all kinds of institutions. Recently, when a new federal courthouse was built on the harbor in downtown Boston, the judges seized all the water-view space for their offices, relegating support folks to interior cubicles. One court employee, quoted in the *Boston Globe* on September 12, 1998, commented, "They're sending us a message: 'This is what we think of you.' It's demoralizing."

Contrast this approach with that taken by Alcoa with the building of a new headquarters in Pittsburgh. Here, space was designed to metaphorically reflect the kind of environment Alcoa wants to create: Everyone in the organization sits in open cubicles—from the CEO to new hires; there is one large cafeteria and no executive dining room; escalators have replaced elevators so that folks can see each other, say howdy, and share ideas. The entire Alcoa building is designed to nurture the learning and relationships critical to business success. The structure sends strong egalitarian messages by eliminating the palatial offices and private dining rooms widely considered standard corporate officer perks.

In recent years, corporate officer pay and perks have increased dramatically in most organizations. Although David Kearns, former Xerox CEO, drove his old, beat-up Chrysler convertible to meetings with other CEOs, corporate officers and their retinues now travel like Middle Eastern potentates in chauffered limos and corporate jets. This isolation is metaphorical for their isolation from the marketplace and the realities of daily life. I was once shocked to hear guys who had just raked in millions in bonuses suggesting that hourly employees' benefits be eliminated to save money. When questioned about the morality of such an approach, one bonehead replied, "There is no place for morality in business." Oh, really? No wonder folks discount these goofballs when they espouse such inane and callous attitudes.

Seniors again hurt their credibility by the company they keep. I'm not saying that there aren't some good-hearted, bright corporate types. There are. But there are also a surprising number with the intelligence of Furbies. When these fools get promoted, it does cause one to wonder about the kahunas running the show. What are they thinking? Or do they just enjoy being surrounded by insufferable toadies?

There are also a lot of mean bosses walking the corporate halls. A pal of mine works for a guy so odious that even his "best friends" hate him. This brute, one of the top officers in a global corporation, also has a nasty shoplifting habit. When anyone inquires about his whereabouts, the usual reply is, "Oh, he's out picking up a few Christmas gifts."

Then, of course, there is the "carryin' on" that is part and parcel of some corporate offices. Those news commentators— the ones whom Calvin Trillin calls the Sabbath gasbags—who proclaimed that if Clinton had been a CEO he'd have been fired for canoodling with "that woman," have obviously not spent much time talking to people in corporations. As far as anyone can tell, some of the big guys see carrying on as droit du seigneur. And they don't get fired for these antics or other inappropriate behavior. One senior was in his cups at a recognition dinner when a buxom young woman walked in carrying a cake. Spying her, he roared, "Why, that cake looks like tits. In fact, it looks like your tits." He was hustled off and temporarily demoted till things simmered down, but he remains at the corporation even now and has a fine job. The boys do love their little club. It reminds me of the line from that old country song, "My wife ran off with my best friend, and I miss him."

There are major problems with expecting organizational change to come from the top of an organization. First of all, it is about as probable as expecting feudal lords to design and embrace a free-market economy. Second, these people are not the future; most of them will be gone in five years. Third, trying to change an organization through the hierarchy inevitably perpetuates hierarchy. Fourth, placing responsibility at the top removes responsibility from everyone else. Fifth, the top doesn't know squat about how to create better organizations. Lord knows, they've spent buckets of money chasing the latest fix du jour.

Programs designed to improve organizational performance have had mixed results at best. Bain and Company, a consulting firm, has tracked usage and satisfaction levels of numerous tools and techniques since 1993, and their research results were published in the September 1998 issue of *Fortune*. They ranked satisfaction with various approaches by subtracting the dissatisfied users from the extremely satisfied users.

Here are their results, drawn from a database that includes 4,137 survey responses and 224 personal interviews with senior managers in fifteen countries.

Satisfaction with Various Methods to Improve Organizational Performance

Method[a]	Extremely Satisfied (%)[b]	Dissatisfied (%)[c]	Ranking[d]
Strategic planning (90%)	28	8	20
Strategic alliances (68%)	26	8	18
Customer satisfaction measurement (79%)	22	6	16
Mission and vision statements (87%)	26	12	14
Pay for performance (78%)	24	10	14
Core competencies (67%)	16	5	11
Benchmarking (86%)	16	7	9
Growth strategies (61%)	17	10	7
Total Quality Management (60%)	16	14	2
Reengineering (64%)	15	16	−1

[a]Percentages in parentheses after each method represent the percentage of 4,361 respondents who use the method to improve organizational performance.

[b]Percentage of 4,361 respondents who were extremely satisfied with the method.

[c]Percentage of 4,361 respondents dissatisfied with the method.

[d]Calculated by subtracting the percentage dissatisfied from the extremely satisfied.

SOURCE: Bain and Company data in *Fortune*, September 1998.

Companies search endlessly for the magic bullet that will solve all problems. We think that the problems are "out there" and that there is bound to be some remedy "out there" that can fix them. Some external situations do affect all of us, but for the most part, our problems are created by our own thinking. Maybe dissatisfaction with all these methods comes from our own expectations. I'll admit that a few of these tools make me want to bang my head against a wall—especially mission and vision statements—but most of the techniques can be helpful when seen for what they are, methods to address specific issues. It's just that none of them will cure what really ails us. What ails us is our inability to critically challenge our own assumptions: all hat and no cattle.

Transforming organizations is not an either/or proposition. It is not either "from the top" or "from the grassroots." It is an and/also endeavor. We have all created our communities together, and it's going to take all of us to re-create them.

We must become aware of the historical belief systems that underlie our assumptions and behavior. Those who have studied the history of patriarchy understand that, fundamentally, patriarchy is about dominance and submission. So is elitism. The problem with all dominance patterns is that they are invisible. If we are to transform our communities, we must make these invisible structures visible. Understanding these tacit belief systems is an ongoing process. Once you begin to see some of the manifestations of patriarchy and elitism, your heightened awareness will lead you deeper and deeper into the structures.

Start watching for *father-knows-best* behavior and assumptions—in others and in yourself. We all have remnants of the belief system because humans have been living in patriarchal societies for centuries now. When you find yourself thinking that managers have all the answers, stop yourself. Remember, managers make up about 5 percent of most organizations. It is not reasonable to believe that 5 percent of the folks have the whole picture.

Don't assume that everyone will interpret information the same way. Your take on information is colored by your role in the enterprise and your life experience. Booming sales are seen differently by marketing types than by the people who have to get the product out the door. Corporations could save billions of dollars if they'd just take the time to get multiple perspectives before taking action.

Be aware of the *let-them-eat-cake* mentality. Elitism is exclusionary, demoralizing, and corrosive. Watch how "class" plays out every day. Elitism is more subtle than patriarchy, and all of us suffer from elitism to some degree. It often manifests as a gap between the espoused theory and the theory in use—like laying people off even as corporate officers make out like bandits. It shows up in statements like, "What does he know, he's only a secretary." George Bush gave himself away when he used "summer" as a verb or when he complained that he lost the Iowa caucus because all his supporters were too busy planning their daughters' debutante parties.

Our Puritan heritage is fairly easy to spot. Anytime you hear someone implying that "suffering is good for us," "this hurts me worse than it hurts you," "this will make you a better person," or "no pain, no gain," it's usually coming from that old Puritan place. It's the guilt-ridden part of us that institutions exploit—the reason some of us feel horrid if we work less than sixty hours a week or take off an hour for a doctor appointment. It's the reason people act so virtuous when they drag into the office with the flu. At XBS, some folks just hated that fun played such a big part in the change strategy. Some hidebound Puritans, despite lots of data to the contrary, just couldn't accept that laughter and fun enhances learning and productivity. It does—so go for it!

Now here's the good news. Several corporate types, including some CEOs, are experimenting with new ways of doing things, disturbing the systems where they live and work. And this is the way we'll create the new workplace—through all of us taking action within our own circles of influence.

One organization taking a number of exciting approaches is Rosenbluth International, a global travel services company with headquarters in Philadelphia. In the travel business, one of the big perks is familiarization trips (known in the business as "fam" trips)—excursions to see new destinations, to become familiar with new conference facilities, or to try out new hotels. At Rosenbluth, managers don't hoard these trips for themselves; instead, all associates get paid time off for "fam" trips, and the company throws in spending money to boot. Rosenbluth focuses mindfully on the culture of the organization. During regular celebrations, the values of fun, learning, meaning, and community are actualized in the moment. Celebration themes abound, but many include the Rosenbluth mascot, the salmon. "The salmon is our mascot because we like to be different, to swim upstream, to buck the tide."

Several years ago a cross-functional group who dubbed themselves the Salmon Spirit Team came up with a number of ways to nurture the Rosenbluth culture. They began by declaring 1996 The Year to Have Fun. They collected ideas from throughout the company on how the organization could support the culture, boost morale, and foster fun. The team also came up with some ideas of its own. The result was the *Salmon*

Spirit Guide, a fifty-page booklet with step-by-step instructions for creating cool celebrations and recognition activities.

The company continually seeks feedback on how they're doing. They regularly send out packs of crayons and paper to a hundred people at a time with the request that folks draw pictures of how they feel about the company. This practice, an ongoing "temperature check," has proved so popular with employees that customers have become part of the process. The drawing project has provided rich insight into the strengths and potential weaknesses of the culture, allowing the organization to learn on the fly in a fast-moving business.

The proof of the pudding at Rosenbluth is their business results, which are spectacular, proving what we all intuitively know: When people feel good, they are more productive. Rosenbluth's people are not afraid to challenge the way things are and do so in every part of the business. And although CEO Hal Rosenbluth sponsors and endorses these new approaches, it is clear that everyone participates in the success of the business. At Rosenbluth, change is an ongoing, systemic process.

In other companies the process of transformation begins with the act of one individual. I was intrigued by the headline on a small story in *Fortune* (October 26, 1998) that read "A CEO Cuts His Own Pay." The CEO featured was John Lauer, who heads up Oglebay Norton, an industrial sands and shipping company in Cleveland. Lauer, whose career background included stints with Celanese Chemical and B. F. Goodrich, found himself with time on his hands while looking for a CEO spot. He enrolled in a doctorate program at Case Western Reserve University's Weatherhead School of Management. He became fascinated with the growing economic gap between the haves and have-nots in corporations and came to two conclusions: CEOs are grossly overpaid, and their obscene compensation is actually eroding loyalty and productivity within their organizations.

When he took the CEO spot with Oglebay Norton, Lauer designed an unusual pay package that is truly tied to performance. For starters, he has worked since January 1998 without salary. During that time, he has spent $1 million of his own money buying Oglebay shares on the open market. He will earn 2.8 percent dividend on these shares plus a performance bonus capped at $200,000. He received a one-time option package—389,174 shares—which vests in 2001. But the options can be exercised at $38, a 25 percent premium to Oglebay's market price the day they were issued. "The way I really make a lot of money is if through my actions and leadership this company can perform in a sustainable way," says the fifty-nine-year-old Lauer. Now, there's a guy willing to put his money where his mouth is. Lauer has bought himself some latitude with the board, who own 25 percent of the shares, plus he's earned the respect of longtime Oglebay people. He also gets praise from financial analysts who understand that although things may get worse before they get better, the turnaround effort is being led by someone with integrity.

This is an impressive story on many levels. First, Lauer has given a lot of thought to the effects of the increasing economic gap—as it affects society at large as well as business enterprises. In his study, Lauer undoubtedly had to examine his own deeply held assumptions about "the way things are." Then, he used his new insights to design a fresh way of doing things. Change happens in the doing, but it starts with the thinking.

Lauer is doing what all managers should be doing: thinking deeply, then experimenting with new ways of acting. He's moving away from a leader-as-manager model to a more organic approach that I call the leader-as-environmentalist approach. Yes, he's still involved in growing the company, but he has taken an action that will have a very healthy effect on the environment of the enterprise.

Lauer proves that the ol' boys can indeed change. Of course, there will be naysayers who will hope that Lauer fails with his new pay plan—particularly people afraid that the idea might catch on and affect their own compensation. But that's small, short-sighted, self-serving thinking.

It's open-minded people who will make a difference in the long run—people who see things differently and are willing to try fresh approaches. In *The Principles of Psychology*, William James reminds us, "Genius . . . means little more than the faculty of perceiving in an unhabitual way."

8

Let's Get Everybody on the Same Page

Life is plurality, death is uniformity. By suppressing differences and peculiarities, by eliminating different civilizations and cultures, progress weakens life and favors death. The ideal of a single civilization for everyone, implicit in the cult of progress and technique, impoverishes and mutilates us. Every view of the world that becomes extinct, every culture that disappears, diminishes a possibility of life.

Octavio Paz

Let's get everybody on the same page! Oh, damn, do we have to? Is this like being good soldiers, team players, singing out of the same hymnal, marching in lockstep, and those other sayings that are tacitly about conformity? Corporate types talk a lot about diversity. Some organizations have even done a pretty good job of creating workforces that are ethnically and gender diverse. But it stops there. Yep, people can be different colors and different genders, and they can even have diverse sexual preferences—on one condition. They've got to think, talk, and act like everyone else.

I'll never forget my first career counseling session with Curt Stiles, then the president of XBS. The session was scheduled shortly after I went to work for him. Curt is smart and a good strategic thinker, so I was expecting deep insights and illuminating ideas. I was flabbergasted when he told me that if I wanted to enjoy continuing success, I'd have to lose my Texas accent. The problem, he explained, was that I was "just too different."

Now, having lived in the Northeast for some years, I was aware of the bias against Southerners, the tendency to subtract fifty IQ points on hearing a Texas twang. This view is not helped by TV news reporters who, when covering events in the South, seem to go in search of folks who sound like the Beverly Hillbillies. And in movies, it is always some Southerner who is a brick short. So when Curt offered to send me to twang school with a local speech therapist, I agreed to go. For once in my life I was unusually compliant. After all, this was the president, and my professional future was in his hands, so I figured I'd better heed his advice. I got caught up in *his reality* because he represented the Xerox power structure. And although I did soften my accent, I ultimately had to decide how much I was willing to conform. The answer was, not that much.

The truth is that corporate systems—the way people are paid, promoted, recognized, and mentored, the lived values of the organization—all have grown out of white male norms. Curt, as part of the power structure, was counseling me to become *more like him* because he understood the system well, he knew how to "get ahead"—by acting like all the powerful white guys.

White male norms are taken for granted. They are implicit. They are encoded throughout the system. The way the white-guy power structure sees the world is "truth." This is not surprising, because institutions—government, the military, academia, and business—have been dominated by white males for centuries. But, as Catharine MacKinnon reminds us, "the world is not entirely the way the powerful say it is or want to believe it is. If it appears to be, it is because power constructs the appearance of reality by silencing the voices of the powerless by excluding them from access to authoritative discourse."

So while the espoused theory is diversity, the theory in use is conformity. Why all the talk about diversity, then? Is it simply political correctness? Intellectually, there seems to be acknowledgment that diversity creates more robust organisms, that *all of us* know more than *some of us*. People also recognize that globalization and rapidly changing demographics will have a major effect on marketplaces and workforces. These trends inevitably will call for organizations informed by multiculturalism.

But at some deep level, we want to have it both ways: We want diversity without questioning our cultural norms; we want innovation and creativity, but we're squeamish about giving up control; we want flexibility and the ability to respond quickly to marketplace changes, but we can't imagine trimming our bureaucracies or simplifying the way we do business. That's why when we talk about change, we need to begin with honest conversations about what we want to conserve. We've got to realize that we can't have it both ways.

Let's imagine for a moment that we truly want to create environments that honor and nurture diversity—not just ethnic and gender diversity, but diversity of worldviews, diversity of thinking styles, different ways of communicating, new ways of doing things. If we really wanted to change, where would we begin?

First, we'd need to take a close look at the lock that rationality has on organizational worldviews. In *Voltaire's Bastards,* John Ralston Saul traces how ideas originating in the Age of Reason have morphed into the technocratic thinking dominant in institutions. This diluted version of rationality, often called the scientific method, glorifies logic, linearity, slicing and dicing information a thousand ways, analyzing systems by reducing them into piles of component parts, measuring things till the cows come home, formulating predictions, and talking about all this in ways incomprehensible to regular folks.

A great example of linearity and reductionism is the Xerox management model, the organization's attempt to nail down its dogma. The central model—needless to say there were more than one—was divided into six categories—1.0 Management Leadership, 2.0 Human Resource Management, 3.0 Business Process Management, 4.0 Customer and Market Focus, 5.0 Information Utilization, and 6.0 Business Results. Each category had a series of subcategories. Here's a sample:

- 2.0 Human Resource Management
- 2.1 Interdependence/Empowerment
- 2.2 Growth
- 2.3 Sourcing and Development
- 2.4 Competence/Skills
- 2.5 Management Development

When I'd talk to seniors about the change strategy, one of them would inevitably ask, "So is what you're doing 2.1 or 2.2 or what?" Then they'd argue among themselves about which bucket was the right one. The change strategy was holistic, integrated, interconnected, and designed to influence every part of the enterprise. So it was impossible to break it down into arbitrarily defined parts.

This management model, incongruent with the complex, dynamic nature of the organization, tacitly communicates a mechanistic view of the enterprise. It is also boring as hell. To quote Anne Lamott, "Rationality squeezes out much that is rich and juicy and interesting."

This kind of linearity and reductionism works for certain kinds of learners and thinkers—it's a day at the beach for people who are very left-brain dominant. But for those who are Gestalt thinkers, who see the big picture and think simultaneously rather than sequentially, this model is totally useless. At Xerox and many other institutions, models like this one are considered the norm, not to be questioned or challenged. The unspoken message is, "This is the way we think here. Like it or lump it."

I'm not saying that there is no call for logic and linearity. But we also must invite deeper ways of knowing, multiple ways of learning, diverse ways of thinking. While quantification and measurement have a place in the scheme of things, the truth is, as Einstein said, "Everything that counts isn't countable, and everything that's countable doesn't count." We need to understand the difference between measuring and knowing. You know how much you love your kids, but you can't measure it. You know how bad your toothache is, but you can't quantify it. And we all know that numbers can lie. Career staffers can manipulate numbers to prove damn near anything they put their minds to.

Voltaire's rationality was a robust approach to critical thinking. Yes, he encouraged the use of factual information. But he also intended that facts would emerge from a rich contextual knowledge of science, history, literature, and the arts; he assumed that we would use critical thinking to pursue moral action; he believed that worldviews would be expanded by weaving all these elements into a textured whole.

We need to broaden our views of rationality, to get beyond the narrow focus on specialized knowledge and our pursuit of tidy answers. We must encourage bigger, deeper, and richer thinking, and to do this, we must overcome the anti-intellectual bias prevalent in institutions. There is no contradiction in being knowledgeable, well read, and even intellectual while being a person of action. We need to foster the exploration of new ideas and fresh perspectives and welcome multiple ways of knowing: the linear and logical (sometimes called "separate knowing") and interconnected, patterned knowing (sometimes called "connected knowing"). The current organizational habit of discounting creative folks as dreamers, idealists, unrealistic, or space cadets—the subtext here is "nonconformist"—marginalizes the very people who can expand and deepen our thinking. This habit of dismissing those who don't fit the mold as impractical extinguishes questioning, curiosity, imagination, and innovation. It establishes a norm of mediocrity. It perpetuates all hat and no cattle.

The second thing we need to consider is the role competition plays in creating diversity-rich organizations. Americans are socialized to be competitive, to believe that competition is inevitable, part of human nature, the way life is. It starts in school with spelling bees and choosing up sides for baseball and pervades our lives from then on. We compete at sports, at board games, at getting into college, and at landing a job, and we enter workplaces structured to foster competition. We believe competition makes us better, makes organizations more productive, keeps us on our toes. Extensive research on competition shows that all these beliefs just ain't so.

The surprising truth is that people are *less productive, less creative, less effective,* less of everything humans can be when they are in competitive situations. And, guess what competition promotes? Conformity. The more people compete, the more alike they become. That's what benchmarking and best practices are about—taking other people's ideas and copying them. Look at what marketplace competition produces. A big Hollywood hit typically spawns numerous sequels and endless imitations. Innovative products quickly are knocked off and repackaged and rapidly become just one more commodity. Can anyone describe the difference between a VCR made by Sony and one made by RCA? The minute an organization hears of a new service being offered by its competitors, it quickly follows suit. Competition doesn't promote creativity, innovation, and risk taking. It kills it.

In organizations, the zero-sum mentality produced by competition—that for me to win, you have to lose—dampens collaborative efforts. If you want to be promoted, the safest bet is to take no risks and to become just like the boss. David Kearns, a former Xerox CEO, tells a great story in his book *Prophets in the Dark.* He describes a Xerox guy whose naked ambition led him to talk, walk, dress, and comb his hair just like Kearns. The two men began to look so alike that Kearns's own kids once mistook the other fellow for their dad.

Competitive environments discourage challenging the status quo. You get along by going along. Think about it; when you wanted a good grade, did you tell your professor his theories were hogwash? No, you were respectful and obedient. The same holds true in organizations. Lots of managers surround themselves with toadies. So if you want to be part of the in crowd, it's risky to be different. A pal of mine recently challenged a yes-man-lover's view of the world. The last time I heard, my friend was on his way to Indonesia—steerage class, in a middle seat.

If we really want innovation, inquiry, creativity, and more effective companies, we need to design organizations that are structurally less competitive. Because of the way we've all been socialized, this is going to be a big undertaking. But humans have created organizational structures and systems, so that means we can re-create them. We will have to approach this issue as we'd approach eating an elephant—one bite at a time.

There are some logical places to start eliminating competition in our lives. We can quit having contests and phase out stacked rankings. We can quit making competition integral to learning experiences. We can quit making individual recognition the centerpiece of organizational meetings. We can quit pitting people against each other. We can begin to notice how competition affects the way we think and act. We can quit asking our kids how their grades compared with everyone else's or whether their soccer team won or lost.

The third thing we'd do is to continue exploring how our mental models about race, gender, and class affect what we do in organizations. We've made progress, but institutions can still be uncomfortable places for women and minorities who exist as "others" in communities where the norms of white males prevail. Actually, enlightened white males feel marginalized as well. The field of multicultural social science is expanding to include whiteness studies. These studies should be helpful because we will begin to understand that white norms do not constitute reality—just one version of reality. We will see how racism and sexism hurt everyone, including those who perpetuate both. Additionally, overlapping explorations of multiculturalism and feminism continue to provoke interesting dialogue about how each informs the American psyche.

The fourth thing we'd do is learn how to have real conversations—not chitchat, not corporate speak, not social niceties. We need conversations in which we begin to understand the words of Camus: "There is no truth, only truths."

We have an unhelpful institutional habit of cramming too many items on agendas, leaving little time for conversation—much less for reflection. Then we rush into gaining consensus on superficially understood issues. The way we use consensus usually shuts down the kind of exchanges that bring multiple viewpoints to the table. As a result, the consensus process is often not helpful in nourishing diversity.

We talk a lot about reflection but seldom do it. We say there's no time. We'd be more effective if we designed our meetings for quality rather than quantity, if we left plenty of space for dialogue. As I mentioned in Chapter 6, we also need to be aware that conversations become difficult with more than four people. Inevitably, side conversations pop up and there is little real listening. At XBS my colleagues and I used to have meetings at our homes. People could wander off and talk in the kitchen, get back together and share ideas, take a lunch break, and allow consensus to emerge over time. We found this approach far more productive than gathering in a conference room with rigid timetables. Some of our best creative thinking happened when we were together this way.

A great tool that we used came from Chris Argyris's work at Harvard. It is called the ladder of inference. The technique is not easy to master but well worth the effort. The ladder of inference looks like this:

Action

Belief

Conclusion

Assumption

Data

Pool of data

Here's how it goes. Each of us continually selects data out of the enormous pool of information that surrounds us. The data we select depends on our life experience, our own mental models. Once we select data, we very quickly make assumptions, draw conclusions, establish beliefs, and take action. We take action on beliefs that are privately held but not publicly tested—and we do it in a nanosecond.

I'll use myself as an example. A few years ago, while in San Francisco on business, I went to a friend's house for dinner one evening. My friend Janis is a gourmet cook, and as I stood in her kitchen watching her prepare dinner, I found myself wishing that I were a gourmet cook. The following evening, I was walking along Union Square, and as I passed Macy's, I spotted a set of Henckels knives in the window surrounded by big red signs announcing, "Sale!"

- My data: Last night at Janis's I noticed a set of Henckels knives on her kitchen counter.
- My assumption: There must be a connection with owning Henckels knives and being a gourmet cook.
- My conclusion: Janis is a gourmet cook *because she owns Henckels knives.*
- My belief: If I own Henckels knives, I'll be a gourmet cook.
- My action: I walked into Macy's, bought three hundred dollars' worth of knives and had them shipped home. I now use them to open FedEx packages.

We all do this countless times every day. We take action without pausing to test our own thinking.

Using the ladder of inference is a way to test our beliefs, to make our logic explicit to others, and to understand the assumptions other people are making. You gain understanding by backing down this ladder.

Here's an example of how inquiry leads to understanding another's thinking: My friend Diane has been married for several years to Bruce, a guy who was so shy that he seldom had serious relationships. One evening she asked him how he got up the courage to pursue her and, ultimately, to propose.

Bruce: "Well, I knew you liked me" (his belief).

Diane: "How did you know that?"

Bruce: "Well, the first time we went out, I noticed a heart sticker on your kitchen calendar" (data).

Diane: "Yes, and . . . "

Bruce: "Well, it marked the day of our first date" (assumption).

Diane: "Then what?"

Bruce: "Well, then I noticed that every month, you put another sticker on the anniversary of our first date, so I figured that was significant" (conclusion).

Diane: "So, if you hadn't seen those stickers, you might not have kept asking me out?"

Bruce: "Probably not."

Diane: "Then it is a good thing you didn't realize that they were reminders to give the dogs their heartworm medicine."

When first using this approach, you'll begin to notice how many assumptions people state as fact.

Jane: "If we take away this customer satisfaction bonus, our account reps won't care about our customers."

You: "Why do you think that?"

Jane: "Well, after we started paying that bonus, our customer satisfaction scores went up."

You: "Oh, so you think the scores were a direct result of the bonus?"

Jane: "Absolutely!"

You: "I thought it was because we finally fixed the billing system that customers have been complaining about for years. It has always been their biggest gripe."

Jane: "Oh, I hadn't thought about that."

Tim: "Actually, I thought the scores went up because we had reorganized the sales force."

You: "Really? How did you draw that conclusion?"

Tim: "Well, I talked to a customer who commented how much he liked his new account manager."

You: "Interesting. Maybe we need to dig into this further."

In the preceding conversation, each person selected different data and drew different conclusions. Rather than taking action based on one person's belief, each shared what he or she thought and why the person thought it—unemotionally. The group made their logic explicit.

This approach focuses on the data we select and the inferences we make—why we believe what we believe. The technique is incredibly helpful and easy to share with others. It is tough to use at first because it is not our habit. If you listen to conversations, you'll hear people arguing from a high level of inference, never pausing to inquire into the reasons for multiple views.

I learned this approach from Bob Putnam at Action Design, a consulting firm based in Cambridge, Massachusetts. Bob and his business partners studied with Chris Argyris. I saw such promise in the approach that we engaged Bob to come into Xerox and teach a number of us this technique. It made a big difference in our team's ability to work together and to coach others. Using the ladder of inference is now such an ingrained habit that I seldom give it a second thought.

When I was first learning this technique, I told Bob that I wasn't sure I'd ever be able to have a normal conversation again. It was so tough not to call people on their assumptions. Bob shared a funny story about Chris Argyris. He said that Chris and his wife were going to a party one evening, and as they approached the door, Chris's wife turned to him and said, "Chris, this is a party, these are our friends . . . and we don't have many left."

Using the ladder of inference or any other thought-provoking technique takes time and patience. But only through inquiry and reflection will we deepen our understanding of diverse viewpoints. Understanding the assumptions underlying current organizational practices is the first step toward creating productive organizations filled with learning, creativity, imagination, energy, fun, and meaning.

As Emerson said, "The world is his who can see through its pretension. What deafness, what stone-blind custom, what overgrown error you behold is only there by sufferance—by your sufferance. See it to be a lie and you have already dealt it a mortal blow."

9

Communication
Is a Thing

Words lead to deeds. They prepare the soul, make it ready,
and move it to tenderness.

Saint Teresa

A journalist friend once described a disastrous meeting at a
large metropolitan paper. Suspicious reporters and editors were
herded into an assembly hall for a presentation on a new benefits package. The messenger was a chipper, very pregnant human resources staffer who opened with a video trumpeting
the advantages of the new benefits—always the first clue that
something is amiss.

When it came time for questions and answers, the reporters
jumped on this staffer like ducks on a june bug. They grilled
her mercilessly, and when she couldn't answer their questions
or tried to dance around them, they let her have it. The
woman was reduced to tears. When word reached the CEO's
office, he called the editor in chief into his office and demanded an apology. The editor reportedly explained, "What
the hell do you expect? These people are trained to spot bullshit from a mile away."

Neither the human resources person nor the reporters were to blame in this situation. The hostility sprang from a culture made dysfunctional by mistrust. The communications approach looked like an attempt to hoodwink the very folks who were valued for their ability to ferret out the truth. In reality, there was no way to perfume this pig. The revised benefits cost more and delivered less. The communications approach was condescending, insulted people's intelligence, and created credibility issues for management. "If they are lying to us about this, what else are they lying about?"

We tend to think of communication as the memos, brochures, and videos that we prepare—the things we do *after* the real work is done. We need to remember that everything is communication: every action, the language we use, the way we engage people, the way we have meetings, who comes to the meetings, who gets promoted, who hangs out with whom, how people are paid, our strategies, the gap between the es- poused theory and the theory in use. *Everything is communication, and communication is everything.*

Although everything that we do is communication, commu- nication is *not* just a "thing." One of the most interesting as- pects of communication is that no matter what you write or say or do, people will interpret it based on their own perspec- tives. We've all had the experience of sending out a memo that we considered self-explanatory and clear as a bell, only to discover that people interpreted it in various ways, that others did *not* find it self-explanatory and clear as a bell. It's impor- tant to understand that meaning is constructed based on peo- ple's life experience, their role in the organization, their social crowd, their work group, and a thousand other variables that we'll never be able to figure out. There is no such thing as per- fect communications or pure information. Words and actions that seem quite clear to you may be construed differently by others. Once you realize this, it's much easier to design a congruent communication strategy that contains redundancies, honors stylistic diversity within the organization, and leaves room for imagination and for the construction of meaning.

Everyone in organizations communicates all the time, and everyone, at the very least, influences the way organizational communications happen. So it's important to understand communications fundamentals.

Let's start with language. Language has generative power. There is a relationship between the words we use and the way we see the world. Our words and metaphors are windows into our mental models. Our thinking and acting are intertwined. One thing we did at XBS was to begin using language and metaphors congruent with natural systems theory, with our beliefs about people, and with the outcomes we desired.

I've already mentioned that even as Xerox talked about a flattened organization and a more participative enterprise, it defined empowerment as "pushing decisionmaking down to the lowest level." "Empowerment" was often discussed as if it were some sort of fairy dust, or a property that could be bestowed. This "pushing decisionmaking down" definition was at odds with what Xerox said it wanted and created an immediate gap between the espoused theory and the theory in use.

As I wrote the initial change strategy, I intentionally used language to reduce dissonance, suggesting that empowerment grows out of organizational conditions—and so does learning. Thus, the strategy was to create an environment where learning and empowerment flourish.

Our change team also began look for alternatives to hierarchical language. It's sometimes tough to figure out how to express the reality of hierarchical organizations in nonhierarchical terms. For instance, I use the term "senior managers" because, to me, it is less troublesome than "top managers." "Top," "bottom," "over," "under," "low," and "high" all connote dominance.

The XBS seniors were known as the Policy Committee. They didn't like the term, nor did anyone else. However, other options were even worse. "Leadership Team" implied that leadership resided within this group when, in fact, leaders emerge from everywhere in organizations and most people can take a leadership role at one time or another. The word "team" would also have been a misnomer; it is well documented that the nature of corporate staffs doesn't lend itself to teamwork. "Committee" was a reasonably accurate descriptor of the way the bunch functioned. "Policy" sounded bureaucratic. The truth was, nobody had any better ideas that satisfied this group. So "Policy Committee" it was. As you consider what to call teams, reflect on whether the words reflect the kind of workplace the group says it wants.

Other words are easier to deal with. Terms like "the masses," "the troops," "the workers," "the bottom" are antithetical if you're trying to create a more pluralistic environment. Why not "the slaves," "the drones," "the drudges," "the underlings," or "the riffraff"? One XBS senior talked so much about "ordinary bears" that we began to play with ideas around "no ordinary bears" and "extraordinary bears." We were continually seeking words that helped to create the future now.

Hierarchy rears its ugly head when it comes to titles. The reason my colleagues and I used the title "learning person" was that it was nonhierarchical and therefore reflective of the workplace we envisioned. Titles communicate. Some titles selected by corporate change agents are surprisingly hierarchical. Hierarchical titles perpetuate hierarchical thinking and acting.

If you're interested in creative titles, check out *Fast Company*'s monthly feature: *Job Titles of the Future.*

We also worked on the language of mechanism, which was tough because our lives are filled with machine language, metaphors, and images. A recent *New York Times* article on the global economy was accompanied by a world map superimposed with the wheels and gears of a large machine. I've seen a number of annual reports using machine imagery—tacitly communicating that organizations are machines and, one could infer, the people cogs.

We are immersed in mechanism. As children, we read *The Little Engine That Could,* and lots of adults have loved Robert Persig's *Zen and the Art of Motorcycle Maintenance.* In fact, one of my favorite lines from that book is "I finally realized that the motorcycle I was working on was myself." Again, more mechanism.

People frequently use mechanistic metaphors when discussing the economy: "the engine of growth," "what's driving sales in this sector?" Warren Buffet, in a *Fortune* article (July 20, 1998), described his own success in mechanistic terms:

> How I got here is pretty simple in my case. It's not IQ. I'm sure you'll be glad to hear. The big thing is rationality. I always look at IQ and talent as representing the horsepower of the motor, but that the output—the efficiency with which that motor works—depends on rationality. A lot of people start out with 400-horsepower motors but only get a hundred horsepower of output. It's way better to have a 200-horsepower motor and get it all into output.

It's not surprising, then, to hear people speak of organizations in mechanistic terms: drive results, rollout, a well-oiled machine, supply-chain management, reengineer, on track, pipeline, wind down, ratchet, get in gear, change the fan belt while the engine's running, screw up the works, step on it, nuts and bolts, rev up, retool, squeaky wheel, jump start, haywire, and on and on.

The problem is that this language creates the impression that the organization *is* a machine. It leads us to believe that we can "get under the hood and fix the sucker." At XBS we looked for ways to describe the organization as a natural, living system. We eliminated mechanistic words from our own language and other communications, and we invited others to do the same. Every time you struggle to find nonmechanistic words, every time you catch yourself saying "drive," it brings you back to the moment. You'll find yourself reflecting, "No, I'm not a machine and neither is the organization—so what other words can I use?" The very act of pausing to consider your language leads you to pay attention to your own thinking, your own worldviews. Changing your own language is a way of shifting thinking.

We also eliminated combative words and metaphors. War and military language abounds in organizations. One corporate group uses the terms "body bag metrics" to describe "the numbers we live and die by." A January 1999 *Fast Company* article likened looking for a job to war—"misfire and you're dead"—and talked about ways to turn your next interview into a "sure kill." Another story in the same issue was titled "The Conference Commando Field Manual," with two accompanying short pieces titled "Guerrillas in the Midst" and "Rules from a Conference Rambo." Now, *Fast Company* is the hippest magazine around, and I understand that metaphors give stories pizzazz. But metaphors influence our worldviews, so we need to be attentive to the ones we use. Fortunately, in the same *Fast Company* issue, an article about Fernando Flores is called "The Power of Words"—it's about treating everything you say as a commitment, about matching your actions with your words. Hooray!

Workplaces reverberate with military jargon: after-action review, uphill battle, beans and bullets, ground zero, command post, plan of attack, front line, the whole nine yards, policy deployment, take command, debrief, take the hill, good soldier, body count, kill rate, the trenches, crash and burn, armed for battle, man your stations, traitor, retreat, campaign, hostage, surrender, propaganda, AWOL, and so forth. Competitive language is also evident: best practices, competitive edge, winners and losers, the race, fast track, game, team player, beat the competition, bumping and shoving, and the like. These words feed the insidious competitiveness of corporate cultures. At XBS we ended up calling best practices "star stuff"—because that's what we humans are made of.

Last but not least, there's corporate speak. Shortly after signing on as a Xerox sales rep, I wrote a tongue-in-cheek glossary of corporate terms. I came across it recently while going through some old files and, interestingly enough, it demonstrates how ridiculous and hypocritical corporate language sounds to a newcomer. Here are a few of my definitions circa 1981:

- *Impact*   a noun used as a verb. "Will this negatively impact your performance?"
- *Do what's best for the customer*   to do what most closely coincides with your comp plan and/or current contests and promotions.
- *Task force*   group assembled to give the impression that something is being accomplished.
- *Shortfalls*   lousy performance.

- *Targets*   what you miss when you have shortfalls.
- *Step-down*   what happens when a person is fired or demoted. He steps down.
- *Downsize*   lay off.
- *Corrective action*   sometimes comes before *stepping down* and *downsizing*. Happens after too many *shortfalls* and *missed targets*.
- *Exposure*   managers talk about this a lot. May mean the same thing as *mooning*.
- *Aggressive*   euphemism for *exorbitant*. "We have a very aggressive plan for 1982."
- *XFM, HRM, MIP, PA, MRP, etc.*   just a few of the acronyms that allow managers to talk for hours without saying anything. Commonly called *speaking in tongues*.
- *To work through*   same as *to work out*. *Working out* has fallen into disuse in this context. *Work out* now means *to do push-ups*.
- *Track to run on*   presumably to some place you should go.
- *Class Action/Affirmative Action*   words that, when used together, are guaranteed to give managers heart attacks.
- *Go down*   appears to apply only to machines and computers at Xerox.

Corporate types get very attached to this kind of language. A young man I know—I'll call him Jim—signed on with a large investment bank after his college graduation. Like many investment banks, this firm hires lots of bright and accomplished liberal arts majors—enticing them with generous salaries and large signing bonuses. Once these young people are in the fold, however, they are expected to become unquestioning corporate drones.

Jim was surprised when partners in the firm called a meeting and announced that there was a serious issue with the communications office. Apparently, some of the communications staffers—former English majors—were editing partners' writing, correcting spelling and grammar and changing corporate speak into plain speak—beautifully articulated plain speak. In the partners' eyes this was heresy; they were determined to find a solution to the problem. After some discussion, the partners decided to fire anyone who edited their writing and to continue firing people until the problem went away. Sounds like that sign hanging in offices throughout the country—" Beatings will continue until morale improves." Jim ultimately quit this outfit. Although he had to return his signing bonus, he said it was a small price for buying himself out of slavery.

A young woman at Xerox could spout corporate lingo till the world looked level. Her language defined her persona; she seemed almost robotic. Although I liked her very much, she was tough to be around because she came across as uptight, judgmental, and stern—one of several folks whom my colleagues and I referred to as the "corporate hall police." When I ran into her shortly before I left Xerox, she looked like a different person. She was more relaxed, happier. I realized after talking with her for a few minutes that she was using everyday language, and I commented on this change. She told me that she had entered an MBA program at the University of Rochester and that the first thing the program coordinator told students—many of whom came from Kodak and Xerox— was that corporate speak was forbidden. The contrast in this woman's demeanor was striking. It affirmed again for me the curious interaction between language and behavior.

It's easy to get swept up in the latest jargon. It's like picking up slang. But some of the lingo is problematic. "Knowledge management" creates the impression that knowledge is a substance that can be managed—rather than an ongoing process of co-creation. "Change management" gives rise to the notion that change is a thing. Change can be created through disturbances within systems, but managed? I don't think so. Several years ago some Xerox managers began using "open the kimono" as an approximate substitute for "sharing information." So someone might begin a meeting by stating, "Today, we're going to open the kimono." A friend commented that he always wanted to respond, "Oh, please don't. It might scare the horses."

Heidegger said, "Language is the house of being." We create the world and it creates us. Our language doesn't simply record reality, it shapes it. Our words both affect and reveal the way we think, and our actions are intertwined with our thinking. I once heard an internationally famous CEO say that he wanted "to go after my employees with a meat cleaver." Even his own executives seemed shocked by these brutal words. It was as if we all got a glimpse of the true person beneath the glossy veneer.

David Bohm thought a lot about the way language contributes to our worldviews and writes about it in *Wholeness and the Implicate Order*. Bohm was concerned with fragmentation—with our tendency to see the world as a collection of pieces instead of as an interconnected, indivisible whole. He believed that the subject-verb-object language structure actually contributes to the notion of fragmentation, of separation, that we "fall unwittingly into the fragmentary mode of functioning implied by the basic structure." Bohm continues:

> The reason for this is not only that the subject-verb-object form of
> the language is continually implying an inappropriate division be-

tween things, but, even more, that the ordinary mode of language tends very strongly to take its own structure for granted, and thus it leads us to concentrate almost exclusively on the content under discussion, so that little or no attention is left for the actual symbolic function of the language itself . . . it is here that the primary tendency toward fragmentation originates. For because the ordinary mode of thought and language does not call attention to its own function, this latter seems to arise in a reality independent of thought and language, so that the divisions implied in the language structure are then projected, as if they were fragments, corresponding to actual breaks in "what is."

Others believe that fragmentation and linearity arise from the structure of the Western alphabet—that the *a,* then *b,* then *c* is the type of form referred to by Bohm—an implicit worldview that influences the way we see things. In *Understanding Media,* Marshall McLuhan posited that more holistic Eastern thought arises naturally because there is no sequential alphabet; thoughts are expressed in ideographs, which "enables them to retain a rich store of inclusive perception in depth of experience that tends to become eroded in civilized cultures of the phonetic alphabet. For the ideogram is an inclusive *gestalt,* not an analytic dissociation of senses and functions like phonetic writing."

There are many contributors to our thinking—words, metaphors, history, as well as language and alphabet structures. But we aren't going to change the alphabet or the subject-verb-object language structure. We do, however, have the power to change the words and metaphors we use.

Consider how language and metaphors influence your thinking. Notice how mechanism, hierarchy, combativeness, and competition are interwoven into news stories, social commentary, economic reporting, and fiction. Be attentive to language and metaphors: how they are used, how they play out in organizations. Consider the kinds of metaphors that are congruent with the workplace you want. Two universal, natural metaphors are the river and the garden. Noticing language and metaphors is like mindfulness practice. It is a gift of the present. It is a way to stop and reflect about what is going on in the moment.

Use fresh language in all personal communications, whether written or spoken. Eliminate corporate speak. Begin looking at advertising, magazine articles, and newspapers, noticing how language is used. Gather ideas for making your own communication more congruent with the workplace you want. Get a dictionary of etymology to understand word origins and root meanings. Other critical tools are an unabridged dictionary and a dictionary of foreign words and phrases. Enriching and expanding your own understanding and use of language is personally rewarding and will heighten your ability to communicate well.

As words and metaphors communicate, so do images. Communications, like learning experiences, need to be designed for various kinds of learners. Learning and communication are essentially the same in that both are designed so that people will know or will be able to do something different. Remember that we all learn kinesthetically, visually, and auditorily and that each of us has preferred ways of processing information. Most corporate communications—written and verbal—are word dependent with images occasionally thrown in as an afterthought, usually in the form of clip art. Although some decent clip art exists, most of it is not found in PC databases. Clip art that comes with PC packages is usually way too obvious. Bag the images of the rainbow with a pot of gold at the end or the gypsy looking into the crystal ball. Use images that expand thinking and imagination.

The old saw "A picture is worth a thousand words" is valid because images can condense words and abstract ideas into a visual sound bite. At XBS, we developed a visual vocabulary that became part of the change-strategy identity. The images expressed the future-now organization. Central to our graphic theme was a group of people representing the folks of XBS. These joyful people first showed up standing in a line across letterhead, scratch pads, mailing labels, and T-shirts. Some were dancing, some were laughing—and they all were happy. We took great care in the creation of this core graphic to be sure that it communicated key messages—diversity, energy, imagination, fun, learning, and meaning. Amid the XBSers stood Albert Einstein. Einstein's presence provoked questioning and conversations.

Why people? Because the strategy was about people. It was about creating an authentic organization where people were valued and truly participated in the business. When we produced a change-strategy brochure called *Working to Learn Together*, our people's faces were on the cover, up close and personal. We humans are fascinated by pictures of other humans, of animals, and of the natural world because they evoke something deep in us—because they are about us, part of us.

As we went along, the images of these XBS people evolved and changed, becoming looser, sketchier, more abstract. The strategy was about change—so if our images had remained static, that would have created dissonance. We also incorporated archetypal symbols—spirals, circles, stars, hearts, hands—into change-strategy graphics. Jung believed that archetypal symbols are part of a universal language. They evoke meanings that arise from the collective unconscious. We found that the graphics—the people, the symbols, the colors—made large abstract notions tangible, provoked conversations, and created room for reflection and flights of fancy. Images and symbols created conversations, giving people the opportunity to construct their own meaning. The graphics disturbed the system in ways that words never could.

We created our own clip art by putting the images on disks and sprinkling them into the organization so that people could use them in their personal communications. XBS folks turned them into screen savers, used them to make decorations and invitations for field events, wove them into presentations, and spread our messages throughout the organization.

Images bring ideas to life far better than words. And, like words, images both reveal and shape our thinking. So images should reflect the kind of workplace you want to create. Imagery is a way to escape "the flatland" of the printed page—as Edward Tufte explains in his terrific book *Envisioning Information.*

The designs we used not only influenced people in XBS but rippled out into the larger Xerox community. When the Xerox annual report appeared with lots of white space, fewer words, and freestanding pictures of Xerox people doing stuff, a friend from corporate communications called to say that the design was influenced by our approach. Our images were also used in a community involvement effort—to create colorful mobiles for children's hospitals. And this is how disturbances work. When they shake up systems, the systems respond in interesting and unpredictable ways.

Although corporate print communications bring to mind that tribute to mediocrity, "I don't know much about art, but I know what I like," the videos take bad design to an even higher level. Most corporate videos are pathetic and send all kinds of unintended messages. I'll never forget the tape made shortly after Curt Stiles, the not-so-former Marine, became XBS president in the mid-eighties. In a misguided attempt to share Curt's vision and establish a "new leadership" model, some genius had the idea to capture Curt talking about the future of XBS.

Now, Curt is a big stiff and any attempt to make him seem approachable and warm was doomed from the outset. Curt was posed at his desk, slung back in his chair, attempting to seem comfortable. As he talked, his eyes darted around nervously. For some reason, his phone rang throughout the taping and each time it rang, he glared at it and then looked faintly nauseous as he resumed speaking. He came across as shifty and disturbed—like the deranged Captain Queeg in *The Caine Mutiny*. The video was a huge hit with the field because it was so hilarious.

I'm not sure what the thinking is behind executive videos. Of the hundreds I've seen, most are dreadful. Directors seem to think that the messages lie in the words, but messages are encoded into the whole design approach. Video has the capacity to use imagery to tell a story. Would you rather watch a video of Larry McMurtry reading *Lonesome Dove*, or would you rather see the movie *Lonesome Dove*? Would you rather hear someone tell you about an NBA playoff game or watch it on TV? It's possible, without blowing production budgets, to lasso the power of video and engage folks in messages.

I've mentioned the videos that we made at the worldwide learning conference X-Potential. They showed XBS people learning, reflecting, and sharing ideas. Yes, the seniors were in the videos—but strictly as community members. Clips from old movies, graphics, and music added humor, interest, and texture. The videos were laced with fresh ideas and new perspectives; they invited viewers to make their own meaning. The tapes conveyed that XBS was a great place to work and that XBS people were the stars of the show—the ones responsible for our success. Contrast this approach with a talking head pontificating that "our people are our most important assets." The videos did not tell, tell, tell; rather, they created the future now.

There seems to be a belief that although customer communications should be well designed, anything for an organization's own people can be haphazardly thrown together. What kind of message does that send? If we want to create enterprises that nurture learning, imagination, and energy, our communications must reflect those qualities. A company's own people are *at least* as important to success as their customers. So internal communications should be as carefully designed as external communications.

And although they sell products and services to customers, some companies have an aversion to marketing ideas within their own organizations. Sales organizations think nothing of buying buckets of banal trinkets to give customers. Yet, make something beautiful to inspire conversations within an organizational community, and technocrats have a tizzy. We need to get over this penny-wise, pound-foolish approach to communications. Effective marketing of ideas and new business approaches to the people who make the business happen just makes sense. It costs much less than relaunching, retraining, or forcing ideas down people's throats—both in dollars and in human terms.

We also need *think sideways* about communication—figuring out ways for information to travel horizontally rather than vertically. The World Wide Web is a great metaphor for what alternative paths might look like. In fact, the Web is a great tool, although it will never replace face-to-face interactions, nor will it replace the tactility and portability of paper. It's like on-line books. They may be useful in some instances. But I would hate to think of a world without "real books." I'd surely miss the look, smell, and feel of a fresh read.

Although printed communications and videos offer powerful ways to create media that are indeed the message, what we do communicates more loudly than what we say. That's why my colleagues and I welcomed the opportunity to help create large group events—whether kickoff meetings, functional meetings, or Camp Lur'ning. It offered the chance to communicate by doing things in new ways.

At the second Camp Lur'ning, for instance, we expanded the idea of a camp store to include a broad array of books and conversation pieces. I went to Rochester bookstores and, using the Xerox corporate discount, bought hundreds of books for both adults and children. Although some were business books, most weren't. We offered many children's books, tacitly communicating that creating a learning environment extends way beyond the workplace. Both the adult and the children's offerings reflected the multiculturalism of XBS. W.E.B. DuBois's *Souls of Black Folks* sold out the first day; our entire stock was almost depleted by day two. I made an emergency trip into Washington to buy more books—and those were immediately snapped up as well. We sold at our cost. The goal was not to make money, but to create the future now and to disturb the system.

We didn't build a fancy bookstore. Instead, we used what we had—tables and Xerox paper boxes turned on their sides to create shelving, a message in itself. The books and conversation pieces drew people into the space—even people not participating in Camp Lur'ning. The Xerox training facility in

Leesburg is used by lots of corporate, nonprofit, and government organizations as well as Xerox folks, so we were just one of the groups there that week. Many non-XBSers wandered over to see what we were up to. A number of them came into the camp store and bought T-shirts, mouse pads, and other conversation pieces carrying XBS messages about people learning. The items were fun, well designed, and high quality and obviously had universal appeal. This is another example of a disturbance that rippled beyond XBS and even beyond Xerox.

Actions do speak louder than words, and unfortunately, this is where many organizations shoot themselves in the foot. At one large multinational where autonomy and self-determination are publicly espoused, a corporate bean counter, royally ticked off over expenses, mandated a new travel policy. Anyone who now wants to take a trip has to get a signed permission slip from the division president or a corporate officer.

Now, this is an organization where everyone travels all the time—including the division presidents and corporate types. The place came to a standstill until folks in the system figured out how to work around the new policy. Now the honchos leave blank signed permission slips on their desks so that people who need to travel can come in and help themselves. This permission-slip mentality totally undermines any talk of autonomy and participation. It's not surprising, then, that this enterprise's employee satisfaction surveys consistently express lack of confidence in senior management. It is also not surprising that the word "empowerment" provokes cynical laughter.

When Xerox began its Quality efforts, it announced that future promotions would be based on "quality behaviors." But, in fact, the corporation continued to promote managers based on their ability to get business results at any cost. This created a tremendous amount of anger within the organization and slowed the Quality effort. Yes, Quality is widely and rightly credited with Xerox's marketplace turnaround. That's not the point. The point is, how much money did Xerox leave on the table because of this all-hat-and-no-cattle approach? And what was the residual damage?

A corporation that recently did an excellent job of matching words and action is Starbucks. In the summer of 1997, three Starbucks people were murdered in a store in the Georgetown neighborhood of Washington, D.C. The Starbucks CEO, Howard Schultz, flew to Washington immediately on receiving the news. He went to the murder site and met with store employees, who were stunned, grieving, and trying to make sense of this tragedy. Schultz hired armed guards for every Starbucks in the greater Washington metropolitan area to ensure the safety of employees and customers. Moreover, he remained in the area for several weeks after the incident, offering emotional support to the local Starbucks community and aiding police in their investigation. Schultz demonstrated through his actions how he values Starbucks people.

Communication is everything, and everything is communication. To create future-now organizations, it is critical that we close the gap between the espoused theory and the theory in use. What we're after here is integrity and authenticity. And although this is a simple concept, it is not easy. Organizations are paradoxical places at best. As hard as we try, it won't be perfect—but perfection isn't even the goal. As Anne Lamott aptly points out in her book *Bird by Bird,* "Perfectionism is the voice of the oppressor, the enemy of the people. . . . Perfectionism means that you try desperately not to leave so much mess to clean up. But clutter and mess show us that life is being lived."

So don't worry about perfectionism or solving all the problems of the world in one day. Just begin noticing whether what you do communicates what you value and what you want to create. Figure out what actions you can take that really do communicate your values. Experiment with closing the gap between your own espoused theory and the theory in use. And enjoy the clutter and messiness that show you that "life is being lived."

10

I'm from Headquarters and I'm Here to Help You

The elements of a marketing effort are not separate elements. They work together often in surprising ways. Advertising is publicity; direct mail is advertising; everything mingles and commingles and virtually everything, done properly, will contribute.

Harry Beckwith, *Selling the Invisible*

When I took the XBS staff job in 1992, there was some method to my madness. I wanted to see if it was possible for headquarters to develop strategies and programs that would actually help the field get more business, become more profitable, and simplify work. At the time, field people were highly skeptical of headquarters because most staff programs, even those that looked good on paper, proved unworkable in the everyday world.

Field managers were constantly inundated with manuals, memos, program and product announcements, new processes, and training packages; however, 95 percent of these initiatives collapsed for any number of reasons—field disinterest, lack of headquarters support, ill-conceived design, sloppy implementation—you name it. Staffers blamed the field, saying that managers were disorganized, lazy, or incompetent; field people saw staffers as bureaucrats out of touch with the business. Because the field–staff interface problem is found in many enterprises, it will be helpful to share what XBS learned. Whatever your role is within an enterprise, the more you understand institutional pathologies, the better prepared you are to deal with them.

As part of an organizational restructuring in 1992, a number of XBS general managers and sales managers were placed in staff jobs to strengthen field focus. Although we all brought field knowledge, there were ingrained staff approaches to program development and implementation—approaches unquestionably adopted by former field people. So although the content of programs became more field relevant, the way we developed, communicated, and implemented new offerings did not. The waste thus continued unabated. Everyone was frustrated.

Consequently, the field–staff relationships became a key focus of the ethnographic study conducted by IRL (see Chapter 3). In one conversation about the IRL project, Curt Stiles, who had become the marketing veep after Norm Rickard became XBS president, asked me if the ethnographers could help us figure out why "nothing works." He and I agreed that other attempts to understand our issues had failed. So we were both willing to shoot craps to try to gain a deeper understanding of the XBS system.

The ethnographers surfaced two key issues around the way we designed and implemented new programs. First, we were lousy at participatory approaches. Although we got field input on new programs, we didn't involve field people in actually co-designing strategies from start to finish. Second, we habitually spent all our program money on design and development, leaving few bucks for communication and engagement. IRL pointed out that engagement should be part of the overall design, that we should be thinking about engagement from day one.

Because my colleagues and I were working with the ethnographers and, at the same time, experimenting with new approaches to learning and communication, we were beginning to think about strategy and program development very broadly. We were weaving fresh ideas about codesign, learning, communicating, and engagement into change-strategy efforts, and other staffers were beginning to take notice. One such manager was John Bergeron, an engineer whose responsibility included developing new service offerings for the XBS marketplace. John and his team were given the task of evaluating the myriad of digital imaging technologies—both Xerox and non-Xerox products—and figuring out which ones could be used to develop innovative offerings for our customers.

The change-strategy team had been kept small by choice. First, having a large staff group would have been antithetical to our purpose—to nurture learning and creative ways of doing things within the XBS community. Moreover, it was a financial decision: Do you spend money on staff salaries or on disturbances? We had made the decision to stay lean, to form partnerships with people within the community, and to invest in disturbances. There were never more than three team members at any one time. When John asked for help, Lynn Robisch, then on the Change Team, signed on as coach—a role later assumed by Diane Phillips, another team member.

John and his able sidekick, Karen Weitzman, were longtime Xeroids, completely indoctrinated in the corporate way of doing things. But having both been involved in suboptimal efforts, they were seeking a better way. What emerged was an approach to product development and marketing that integrated everything we'd learned—codesign, learning, engagement, communication. John, Karen, and the rest of their group—known as the Einstein Team—took an entirely new approach that paid off big time.

First of all, the team used a process of true codesign, involving field people in every stage of developing an offering called Virtual Printroom Services (VPS). This solution allows manufacturing designers to access, print, and alter engineering drawings digitally, eliminating the handling, duplication, and transport of large, cumbersome documents. Xerox had erred in the past by announcing digital offerings prematurely, without thinking through system compatibility issues, the economic viability of digital solutions, how new services should be marketed, how people would get paid, the kind of infrastructures required, and so forth. Services that looked great on paper were fraught with unanticipated problems, resulting in dissatisfied customers and disgusted field people. The field was sick of beta-testing new offerings on customers, of having to take up the slack for half-assed staff work.

John and Karen invited a group of field people to help design an offering from the ground up, to help the staff think through all the implications of launching a service designed for a new market niche. To be successful, Virtual Printroom Services would require thorough understanding of how engineers get their work done; then, XBS would have to figure out how to configure appropriate software and hardware to meet those needs. Additionally, this offering would require a whole new skill set for XBS associates, the folks who produce the work at customer sites. Furthermore, sales reps and managers would have to learn how to sell the new offering. And the Einstein Team would have to decide how to price and bill services that were outside the traditional XBS model.

The field team members reflected the XBS population: Some were from sales, some from production, some from administration, and some were from other Xerox divisions. Because these folks brought multiple perspectives, they asked questions and raised issues that staffers might have missed. And between meetings with John and his team, the field representatives talked with their pals back home, simultaneously getting input and creating buzz about the new service.

The field people pointed out that in the past, new offerings had little or no support during launch, either in the field or at headquarters. The team began to develop a list of success criteria—the elements essential for the new service to be successful. One requirement was that each field operation would have to dedicate one person to supporting the Virtual Printroom Services introduction.

The team voiced the need for strong, ongoing staff support—an issue also highlighted in the IRL study. XBS had a habit of throwing new services into the field, then having nobody available to answer questions or to support the service on an ongoing basis. In fact, when field people called headquarters with program questions, they often got some confused person on the phone who said, "I'm new. Joe has moved into another job—so I don't know what to tell you." XBS was in a very profitable division. It makes one wonder how profitable we could have been if we'd done things well.

The success criteria evolved into requirements that field operations had to meet if they wanted to offer Virtual Printroom Services in their marketplaces. To qualify as a launch site, field operations had to commit to dedicating one person to support the new service and to holding a large learning event within forty-five days of launching. They were required to develop a list of hot prospects and to demonstrate that they had the infrastructure and people with appropriate knowledge, skills, and attributes to support the Virtual Printroom Services. Nobody was forced to offer the new service; they were just informed that it would soon be available. Funny how people respond when they have a choice in the matter. Field operations clamored for VPS.

Some of the enthusiasm arose from the buzz that the Einstein Team had their act together. The team had followed a detailed process to ensure that the offering was truly field-ready prior to launch. Several customers had such pressing need for the virtual print room that they installed early and became, in effect, learning sites. The Einstein Team gathered useful lessons from these early adopters and incorporated this knowledge into the final offering. Throughout the development cycle, Einstein Team members talked with colleagues throughout the organization, met regularly as a group, and remained open to all feedback and ideas. They set up a Web site, where they published updates, market research data, new ideas, and recent discoveries—and they made this information available to everyone in the organization.

Once the first launch sites were identified, the Einstein Team scheduled the first learning event. The learning approach was similar to Camp Lur'ning in that a group of field folks gathered in Leesburg, participated in a camplike approach to learning, returned to the field, and held their own learning events.

Each operation had a "guardian angel" from the Einstein Team. Guardian angels were available to support learning events, customers, selling activities, installation and infrastructure needs, and whatever else field people required to be successful.

The Einsteins developed a VPS field kit—available in both physical and virtual form—that supported every aspect of learning, sales, implementation, and ongoing operation. They also followed up with the *VPS Idea Book,* described as "a strategic continuous learning resource for an ever-expanding community of practice that began with the Einstein Team's vision. This book includes a growing collection of principles, real-life approaches, suggestions, and stories that accelerate and enhance anyone's ability to create and sustain successful VPS learning experiences in the operations."

The team hired a consultant to administer ongoing surveys of XBSers to determine their satisfaction with every aspect of Virtual Printroom Services—from the way it was researched, developed, and introduced through learning events and the quality of ongoing staff support. The team monitored external customer satisfaction through continuous field feedback and through Xerox's customer surveys.

In effect, the way the Einstein Team operated became part of both the internal and the external marketing effort. They were open and flexible; they made their logic explicit; they co-designed with the field; they involved customers in learning experiments; they designed vivid communications and support tools; they organized energetic learning events that created excitement and pull for their service; they treated everyone they dealt with like customers.

It isn't surprising that Virtual Printroom Services exceeded all expectations for new installations, revenue, profit, and customer satisfaction. The Einsteins are future-now people. There was no gap here between espoused theory and theory in use. The team modeled the kind of thinking and acting that they hoped for in others. They wove the outcomes they wanted into what they did every day. They took advantage of what we had learned about learning, of our experiences with X-Potential and Camp Lur'ning, and of new communications approaches. They used quality tools and processes to develop their approach. They took advantage of research: the ethnographic study, marketing data, and benchmarking information. They developed "ways of knowing" that included both qualitative and quantitative measures. There's a story that illustrates what the Einsteins did not do:

A little girl walks up to a man holding a dog.
"Mister, does your dog know tricks?" she asks.
"Of course my dog knows tricks," he answers.
"Can I see him do some tricks?" she asks.
"Oh, he doesn't actually *do* tricks. He just *knows* them."

The Einsteins *did* the tricks—they didn't just know them. Unfortunately, there are people who can see new approaches, learn about fresh ways of doing things, yet never apply what they learn. These individuals sit down at the beginning of a new project, remember the way they approached their last project, write an action plan, and are off to the races.

The Einsteins began with open minds, were willing to get outside their comfort zones, welcomed diverse views, learned through experimentation and reflection, accessed every resource they could find, and worked their hearts out. And in addition to launching a highly successful service, they experienced personal growth and found meaning in their work. These folks are servant leaders.

Diane Phillips, credited by the Einsteins as bringing creative genius to the team, was involved in several other noteworthy projects that illustrate how to take same-old, same-old corporate programs and turn them into something fresh. We used to tease Diane about being such a soft touch that she ended up with some real doggy projects. Diane had been blessed with "solving" the customer-problem-resolution process—an issue that had been kicking around headquarters for years. XBS had no way to identify patterns of customer complaints, create systemic solutions, or track problem resolution. This project had been tossed from one staff manager to another. Nobody could get support for tackling the core issues, so it went unresolved until it could be passed off to another unsuspecting soul. Finally, it landed on Diane's desk.

After doing some digging, Diane found that everyone who had analyzed the issue had come up with the same results. Customers had two major problems with XBS. The first was the billing process: Xerox's abominable billing system produced invoices that read "March outsourcing . . . $62,000." Customers wanted a little more detail. The true fix for billing had to be done at the corporate level. Customers had been complaining about Xerox bills at least as early as 1981, when I arrived there. By the time I left in 1997, the billing system was as bad as ever. The way XBS field people kept customers satisfied was by manually generating detailed invoices—a major workaround.

The second customer issue was that XBS had no national customer-problem-resolution process. Although local managers had closed-loop processes, XBS had many national accounts that crossed operational boundaries; consequently, the call for a way to resolve problems at the organizational level. Diane's task was to figure out how to fix this issue.

Diane likes statistical analysis about as much as she likes ramming sticks in her eyes, so she engaged a quality consultant, who was also a Baldrige examiner, to analyze customer complaints. This was good thinking because Norm Rickard was a Baldrige examiner and therefore credited other examiners with wisdom far greater than common mortals.

After much analysis, the consultant observed that XBS had no discernible patterns of customer complaints, that the variability of XBS did not lend itself to unitary solutions. Except for billing, problems were highly situational and could only be resolved at the local level. Hooray! Just as we suspected. That was exactly the message we had been trying to get across—that the XBS business was a relationship business, problems had to be dealt with one on one, and headquarters needed to support individualized approaches rather than trying to force standard solutions. The problem that cried out for a corporate solution was billing.

Eventually, Diane wrote the fable "We're Respondable," which we introduced at Camp Lur'ning. Campers wrote their own endings to the fable and, in the process, developed workplace principles that would give rise to customer satisfaction. "We're Respondable" recognized that any headquarters-imposed process was doomed to failure, that customer satisfaction grew instead from our organizational environment, and that our environment springs from our own daily behaviors.

In 1997, Diane was assigned to represent XBS as part of a corporate initiative called XTeams. Although this sounded like an honor, in truth it had great potential to be another thankless effort. The corporation had been struggling to find a way to encourage empowerment without changing any of its command-and-control tendencies. Naturally, an "empowerment model" had been developed—does the world really need another model?—and, not surprisingly, the response was a giant yawn.

Paul Allaire, Xerox's CEO, had been playing with the idea of replacing Team Excellence, an annual gathering where high-performing teams are recognized, with a program called

Xteams, which would award dollars to certain "empowered teams." Paul's idea was vague and was still based on the notion of empowerment as a property, so it remained just that, an idea. Finally, ticked off that nobody was taking his idea seriously, Paul declared, "Let there be XTeams." A task force was convened, with Diane Phillips as the XBS representative.

Diane describes the gathering as typical Xerox—no money, no authority, no imagination, a mandate, a deadline, old ideas, and lots of nice people. The corporate dweeb running the show had come up with a scheme for raising money. He had designed "empowerment" posters and some other dreary materials to sell to the divisions. He went around the room asking how many each division wanted to purchase. When he got to Diane, she said that we wouldn't be needing any. Immediately, most other folks said they wouldn't be needing any either.

Diane returned discouraged because our work had moved us into a new way of thinking about initiatives, one that was incongruent with the rest of the corporation. One staffer suggested that Diane find some old program to dust off and recycle instead of dedicating great effort to what seemed like a doomed initiative. But Diane refused. She was convinced there was a way to design an XBS XTeams approach that would be complementary with the change strategy and would help the organization.

Diane's task was doubly hard because, at the time, travel was restricted and there was no budget for XTeams. The good news was that the corporation was willing to award ten thousand dollars to a maximum of ten teams per division. This is a significant amount of money, especially for the XBS associates who have daily contact with customers. It was an interesting way to test our assumptions about reward and recognition. It was also another way to create new relationships across functional and

geographical boundaries, to further conversation about environmental issues, and to acquaint folks with the actions that individuals could take to change the workplace as we knew it.

Diane assembled a group of field and staff people to codesign the XTeams approach. She was heartened and amazed
at people's willingness to help, which affirmed, once more,
that folks find time to work on meaningful projects. The team
met by telephone and, over several months, developed a
process for communicating, forming, identifying, and recognizing XTeams.

First, the entire initiative was invitational. Field operations
were not required to participate. Neither were teams required
to become XTeams.

Second, XTeams identified and qualified themselves. Any
group could become an XTeam just by proclaiming itself an
XTeam, using guidelines and assessment methods suggested in
the XBS XTeams communication package. XTeams could be a
functional group, a cross-functional group, or a virtual or project group.

Third, each group that wanted to nominate itself as a Division XTeam selected a peer leader. The peer leaders of competing teams acted as judges of XTeam entries. They evaluated
and gave feedback to other competing teams in open telecon-
ferences.

Diane and the guiding team created the future-now organization in the way they defined XTeam processes: self-
identification, self-assessment, peer review, lateral
communication trails, an approach based on relationships—
not hierarchy.

The outcomes were extremely interesting. One thing we had
noticed during Team Excellence presentations was that seniors
didn't give constructive feedback to teams and they deliber-
ated in secret to select winners. The peer review process for

XTeams, on the other hand, was open and completely honest. Peer leaders felt free to comment and offer constructive feedback and were capable of doing so because they, unlike the seniors, had firsthand knowledge of how the work really gets done. Although peer leaders were extremely blunt and held each other to high standards of performance, XTeam representatives were grateful for group feedback and used it to improve their team's processes—either the way they did their work, the way they measured it, or the way they structured their teams.

Peer leaders were diligent about sharing what they were learning with team members who were not part of the "judging process," so innovative ideas began to spread through XBS at the grassroots. What became apparent was that people didn't have to ask permission to take new approaches.

The peer leader group was nonhierarchical—as was the guiding team. Everyone participated as an equal, regardless of the person's spot on the organizational chart. A community of practice arose that was nongeographical, nonhierarchical, and not related to function. The group process created the future now.

Even inside large bureaucracies, it's possible to take "official programs" and turn them into something creative, something that fosters a meaningful workplace. When I give speeches, people often comment that they are bound by the conventions of their organizations and find it difficult to incorporate new ideas. To that I say, just look at what you do every day and identify a few changes that would make the tasks more fun and more rewarding for you and your colleagues. If you are a staff person, here are some ideas to consider when developing new programs for your field organization.

Consider a new initiative from the perspective of participants. Will it be seen as a program that simplifies life and enhances productivity, or will it be viewed as more corporate flimflam?

Get field people involved in codesigning the initiative from start to finish. This will increase your chances of success by a factor of one thousand.

Experiment with implementation in a real-life situation. Will this initiative require local adaptation, or can it be applied uniformly throughout the system? Staffers are prone to assume much more neatness and conformity than actually exists in field organizations. Don't be afraid to bag an initiative that isn't helpful to the field. They'll bag it anyway if you don't. It's called the pocket veto.

Make engagement a key step of the development process, and set aside money and time to do it right. Design learning experiences and communications that honor the way people really learn.

Create a way to use workplace feedback to improve, refresh, and redesign programs. This will require design team members who are willing to shepherd the program after its initial implementation. All too often, staffers throw initiatives into field organizations, then walk away. That is a big cause of organizational waste.

Make you logic explicit. When people question why you are taking a different approach, one at odds with organizational norms, share your new ideas about design, engagement, communication, and learning. If you incorporate ideas from the projects cited here, your results will speak for themselves. Perhaps the next time your colleagues begin designing a new program, they'll come to you for advice.

That's the way change happens—when individuals fatigued with the status quo take responsibility for doing things in new ways. The writer Fran Lebowitz reminds us, "Every intention, every achievement has come out of dissatisfaction, not serenity. No one ever said, 'Things are perfect. Let's invent fire.'"

11

We Supply
Information on a
Need-to-Know Basis

> Any information can become knowledge if a user finds
> it useful or interesting. So, for a business, knowledge
> is any use of information that helps the organization.
>
> **Michael Dertouzos**

Information on a need-to-know basis is another old corporate
saw. What it usually means is, "I'll tell you what I think you
need to know." This philosophy really backfires because attempts to control data and hoard information produce crazy
systems—systems that won't supply critical information when
you really need it, but sometimes spit out surprising confidential data.

Corporations have been shortsighted about information
technology—as evidenced by the year 2000 (Y2K) issues—and
unrealistic about the kinds of investments required to design
user-friendly systems. Unfortunately, many corporate managers recoil from contact with technology. I've known a few
who can't even send a fax. This lack of familiarity and the as-

sumption that technology is some kind of alchemy spawns the belief that any changes ought to be quick, easy, and cheap. Talking to a Y2K guru recently, I did an imitation of the reaction I imagined he was getting in corporations. I waved my hand as if I was sweeping away dirt and whined, "Can't you just fix it . . . and it won't cost more than a dollar, right?" The guru replied, "You've been there."

Information technology *at its best* is a tool that supports innovation, learning, and participatory environments. Although it is not *the* answer, information technology is certainly an important part of the equation.

There is wide variation in the *what*s and *how*s of information sharing across the business landscape: A few companies proclaim themselves "open-book organizations"; others hold all information so tightly that their folks have to read newspapers to figure out what's up. Most enterprises haphazardly share some "official version of the truth," packaging the numbers and spinning the story for general consumption.

At Xerox, it was difficult to tell where truth lay. I do know that the more access I had to numbers and the more analysis I did, the less I trusted the official version of reality. Xerox information systems are a disaster, and although I originally thought that the chaos was typical of a forty-year-old organization trying to manage information with a combination of legacy systems and mushrooming new technologies, I began to wonder if the mess was intentional. Sorry information systems are a fine way to disguise what is really going on in an organization. I have come to believe that Xerox's systems—like those I see in other enterprises—arise from a combination of incompetence, guile, and all hat and no cattle.

Shortly after I became a staffer, I was asked to fill in for a guy responsible for territory design and sales compensation. Unfortunately, it was during the annual planning cycle, so the Marine (the president, Curt Stiles) told me to figure out how to configure sales territories for the upcoming year. Of course, I had no idea what to do. I quickly roped a friend into helping, and we grabbed a college intern to crack the information systems.

We wanted to begin by determining how many sales reps there were by location, so we asked the intern to query the system. We never did get the sales rep numbers. We had to figure them out by getting a bunch of reports, taking bits of information from each, and then calling the field locations to see if we had it right. What we did get, however, was a long list of folks—general managers, sales managers, staff managers—and all their salaries. Naturally, we spent hours poring over this confidential information, complaining over who made what.

Then I started trying to decipher the previous year's planning methodology. When I asked a colleague how base budgets were calculated, he said, "Oh, there was no science. That three-million-dollar base per territory—we just made it up." I was fried because I remembered how hard we had worked to design territories with a $3 million budget. I was also stunned that there was no basis for the assumptions, which made me wonder about the current year's planning approach.

The planning assumptions, already published to the field, stated that certain territories would have 30 percent growth targets for the coming year—that's 30 percent over the previously made-up $3 million. This is called "adding insult to injury." Anyway, I started fiddling around with the numbers by operation and discovered that whereas some locations' budgets reflected a 30 percent growth, others were being assigned 50 to 70 percent growth numbers. Even more surprising, a few operations had numbers representing a 35 percent *decrease* in revenue. I found this curious. As a field manager, I had been highly skeptical about planning methodology, and this information confirmed my suspicions that something was rotten in Denmark.

I did some marketing analysis and could find no logic in the variances. I came across some confidential data left on a copier that made me even more uneasy. Things were as clear as mud. I went to the finance group, showed them my analysis, and witnessed "the dance of the ants"—nervousness, evasion, and weasel words. So I talked to one of the program managers, explaining what I had discovered. He said, "You need to take this to Curt."

Innocent as a lamb, I went to the slaughter. I figured this whole thing was a terrible mistake and that the Marine would be glad I'd discovered the error. Geez, was I wrong. When I detailed my findings, the cowboy about popped a vein. He demanded to know why I was looking at the numbers "that way." I explained that I was just messing around, trying to make sense of the methodology. When he began making veiled threats about my future, I dropped the information on his desk and vamoosed.

I've never figured out whether he was angry because he didn't catch the error, because the finance people goofed, or because "the fix was in" and I caught it. He really made my life miserable for a while; I was pretty sure I was a goner. But I survived, and finance fixed the numbers to be consistent with the published assumptions. But here's the real kicker. Another senior who knew about this blowup asked, "Why do you care if the plans are consistent? What difference does it make to you?" I tried to explain that these numbers have an enormous effect on people's lives, on how they get paid, on how they get treated. Plus, I didn't want to be part of a big lie. This senior had never worked in the field and couldn't understand my concern.

I learned a couple of good lessons. First, planning is baloney. The value of planning is not "The Plan." The planning process is useful only to the extent that it is thoughtful, that it provokes questioning and causes people to challenge old thinking. Second, never accept numbers at face value. Third, be very particular when choosing a boss. Fourth, if you need to find out confidential information, ask an intern or the secretaries. They are the ones who can get the real skinny. Fifth, always look at papers left on copiers and in printer trays. You never know what you'll find. My beliefs about corporate planning, information, and hierarchy are reflected in a document that circulated through the business world a few years back:

In the Beginning Was the Plan

And then came the Assumptions

And the Assumptions were without Form

And the Plan was completely without Substance

And darkness was upon the faces of the Workers

And they spake amongst themselves, saying:

"It is a crock of shit and it stinkith."

And the workers went to their supervisors, and sayeth:

"It is a Pail of Dung, and none may abide the Odour thereof."

And the supervisors went to their managers, and sayeth unto them:

"It is a container of Excrement, and it is very Strong,

such that none may abide it."

And the managers went to their directors, and sayeth unto them:

"It is a vessel of Fertilizer, and none may abide its Strength."

And the directors went to their AVP and sayeth:

"It contains that which aids plant growth, and it is very Strong."

And the AVP went to the VP and sayeth unto him/her:

"It promoteth growth, and it is very powerful."
And the VP went unto the President, and sayeth unto him/her:
"This powerful new plan will actively promote the growth and
efficiency of the department, and this area in particular."
And the President looked upon the Plan, and sayeth that it was good.
And the Plan became Policy.

I came to headquarters with a different philosophy about information. What I had learned as a general manager was that the more we shared, the more everyone understood the dynamics of profit and loss, and the more open we were with data, the better we did. I spent a considerable amount of time with our production people because, frankly, their concerns were often ignored in an enterprise with a strong marketing culture.

These people were dedicated to making the business a success and often came up with good ideas for increasing revenue and profits. I remember meeting with a group that wanted to acquire some new engineering equipment. I encouraged them to track the requests they had for engineering work so that we could use that data to cost-justify the new machines. Several months later, we sat down together and analyzed the numbers. It turned out that the volume of work was insufficient to support new equipment, but the group gained new insight into financial dynamics. I saw them come alive as they worked with the information; they were intrigued and energized. It was quite magical. Their response convinced me that we needed to intensify our efforts to share detailed financial data and teach people how to use it to inform everyday activities.

The philosophy held true for human resource information. In Pittsburgh, racial tensions bubbled under the surface all the time. Minorities in our operation felt underrepresented and overlooked. In an effort to have open and honest dialogue, we assembled demographic information on the Pittsburgh area and gathered raw demographic data on the local XBS population. By raw data, I mean we didn't use any "official data" with its taint of corporate voodoo. We had an actual list of everyone in the operation and the jobs they held. We sifted through the material together. People could take the information away with them, check the accuracy of the data, and bring questions the next time we got together. This effort opened up a dialogue on racial issues; we talked from information that we all agreed was factual. Actually, we were doing a good job of creating a workforce and management team that was diverse in ethnicity and gender, but the issue was perception—the feeling that things were not fair. Frank conversations and willingness to share unedited information created a new level of trust.

I had long questioned how Xerox calculated "balanced workforce" numbers. The corporation factored ethnic representation using an unexplainable methodology purportedly representing the minority population that met corporate hiring criteria. So, for instance, if the Latino community in Dallas constituted 35 percent of the population, Xerox numbers might be factored to a lower number—like 18 percent. Xerox would claim that only 18 percent of the Latino population were potentially available for our workforce. If it sounds weird, rest assured that this kind of mumbo jumbo always sounds strange to nontechnocrats. To me the only thing that made sense was to recruit a workforce that absolutely mirrored the population and to carry this reflection through the entire organization. It is not enough to have all diversity represented within the nonexempt population, for instance. This strange reporting system was why we avoided corporate witchcraft in favor of data obtained from community sources.

As we designed the change strategy, the learning experiences were really about creating a business context, encouraging curiosity, inspiring questioning, and nurturing a new threshold of consciousness. Much of the information that people needed to make sound business decisions could be located, although it wasn't always easy. XBS field managers do lots of number crunching and generally analyze financials to the account level. Good businesspeople—and most XBS field folks are—can always tell you where they're making money and where they are only marginally profitable.

So we knew if we encouraged people to go digging, the revenue and expense numbers could be assembled—even if it was done manually. And although we initially heard some management concerns about sharing detailed account information, the noise had died down by the second year of camp. Field managers told me that they were heartened at the way XBS people dealt with sensitive financial data. I was not surprised, because this had been my own experience.

Organizations that espouse a desire for innovation, flexibility, learning, and participation need to get off the dime and open their books. In conversations with people throughout the business world, responses to the idea of opening the books and sharing information sound like this:

"Our employees couldn't handle that information. Maybe someday, after we train everyone, we'll start sharing."

"We can't do that because somebody might give the financials to our competitors."

"I think it would cause legal problems with our union."

"It would cost too much money to design the systems."

"Isn't that against the law?"

"They don't need that information. It would just confuse them."

"Anyone who needs that information can just go to Finance and get it."

"Oh, we already tell people what they need to know."

"If I share what I know, I lose my competitive advantage."
These dogs don't hunt. The comments are typical in fear-based enterprises, where assumptions are based on scarcity, competition, control, and risk aversion. Even people with access to information, as I was at Xerox, find that it is often fragmented, incomplete, and confusing. What is called for are integrated systems embedded with learning, systems that create meaningful context: What does the whole picture look like? How do I fit? How can I participate and contribute to my fullest? How can I use this data to do my job better? What ideas do I have that can heighten the success of the whole enterprise?

I'm for sharing all information—including salaries, budgeting methodologies, financials—and in a way that enables deconstruction, de-layering, and demystifying the numbers. The only information that should be private is personal data: marital status, medical information, age, number of children, and so forth. Everything else would be available to everyone and in a format that fosters learning.

It is not enough to summarize revenues, expenses, and profits. People must be able to analyze what feeds these numbers. Where did the revenues come from: by marketplace, by operation, by product type? and so on. Expenses should be detailed in a comprehensible and straightforward way. So if I'm a field person, I can see just how much the finance organization is spending on bean counters. And, if I'm really curious, I can de-layer this information and see how many bean counters there are, who they are, and how they get paid. If I want to see what they spent on travel, I can access that information. If I have a question about any of the numbers, I can go to "help" and find definitions, explanations, and methodologies. This is what I mean by embedded learning. Systems can simultaneously provide information and create practice fields for learning in the work context.

At XBS, there was fairly detailed information on field operations, but headquarters expenses were all mushed together and tough to analyze. That's why, as a staffer, I got so incensed when the seniors beat on the field to cut head count, saying we had a serious SAG problem. SAG refers to expense—mostly head count—not directly related to producing work for customers.

XBS's SAG problem wasn't in the field; it was in the burgeoning staff organization—and that analysis had been conducted and shared with seniors. Although everyone knew who had the SAG problem, field managers didn't have access to the information needed to put this issue on the table. One disgruntled senior, an old-time XBSer who understood the business, described the mushrooming staff this way: "Every day, a big yellow bus pulls up in front of XBS and a whole bunch of new people flock into the building. What in God's name are they all doing?"

This kind of one-way information system is dishonest and hypocritical, especially in enterprises espousing management by fact. If your organization conducts its business this way, make some noise. Open-book systems must be open across the board, and every single person in the enterprise should have access to the data, preferably on-line. Naturally, people must learn how to use the information—either through learning embedded in the system itself, a simple game or simulation, or team coaching experiences. Most managers overestimate the complexity of financials. Anyone who has kept a personal checkbook and paid bills already understands the basics. Einstein had it right when he said, "Everything should be made as simple as possible, but not simpler."

Ideally, there should be multiple paths to educating oneself on financials. Reference material and clarifying definitions embedded within financial systems will enable people to learn on the fly. One of the principles of the change strategy was that although people don't have extra time, they do have discretionary energy and creativity. When people find meaning and have fun at work, they are more productive. One of the first steps to creating meaningful workplaces and to accessing discretionary energy and creativity is to nurture business understanding throughout the entire community.

Information sharing via technology also has potential to enable problem solving among natural communities of practice—although technology will not replace face-to-face conversation. Hewlett Packard (HP) has software that allows two thousand researchers from all over the world to enter a professional profile. This helps HP folks locate expertise when they need it. They also have a monthly virtual conference for their two thousand mechanical designers. Using a combination of phones, video, and the Web, participants share designs in three-dimensional and real time. HP folks say that these conferences have led to new designs of exceptional quality.

British Petroleum (BP) experimented with two-way video conferencing technology as a way of reducing travel expenses and found that as people participated in these meetings, they started to build relationships. After sharing information and talking via video, people begin saying, "We have to get together." BP's travel expenses actually went up.

This is not surprising. To understand enterprises as organisms is to know that the organizing principle of natural systems is relationships—not things. So technology that promotes relationships strengthens the fabric of the entity—for better or for worse. The risk is that old thinking gets perpetuated. However, using technology to facilitate relationships at the periphery has potential to foster the kind of innovative environments that we say we want.

Ideally, technology should enable anyone within an enterprise to set up a chat room or a Web page for sharing issues. Chat rooms and other technologies will strengthen relationships only if accurate information is readily available. Nature abhors a vacuum. Institutions are rife with gossip and rumor because, lacking information, people speculate as a way of making meaning. I recently talked to a friend who was in the midst of his 1,700th organizational restructuring, asking him how it was going. "Well," he said, "we're into our typical four-month period where nothing gets done. People are paralyzed by fear. Nobody knows what's going to happen, so nobody's doing squat. We're just calling each other to trade rumors."

Some technologies are a mixed blessing—like voice mail and e-mail. Misused, voice mail and e-mail feed our institutional addiction to meaningless activity—an addiction that creates busywork, values busywork, and confuses it with the real thing. An enlightened corporate change agent describes the day she spent with a senior team. Their purpose was to reflect on the work issues, relationships, and mental models that were hampering group effectiveness. This team, a fearful bunch, decided to work on communication issues. They complained that they were so busy they couldn't even clear their daily e-mails. The group was miffed when their perky administrative assistant chirped, "You know, I've done some analysis on your e-mails, and only fifteen percent come from people outside this group. Eighty-five percent of your messages are to each other."

Most organizational e-mail systems are filled with announcements for birthday parties and showers and complaints about the dirty kitchen. Xerox e-mail was a constant source of entertainment.

A group of Xerox people organized a wonderful project called Sample Soap. Because so many of us traveled, we were encouraged to pick up shampoo, soap, and other sundries from hotel rooms and place them in office collection bins for donation to homeless shelters. It was a great idea, and travelers responded enthusiastically. From time to time, we'd receive detailed e-mails reporting Sample Soap results. Some trickster wrote this takeoff on Sample Soap reporting and distributed it via e-mail:

Sample Smarts Sets New Record

I am happy to report that we have collected a record number of Sample Smarts during this quarter. Over 2,135 IQ points were donated to Sample Smarts for our ongoing work with the intelligence-challenged.

As a result of everyone's chipping in spare IQ points, we have made real progress in our effort to eradicate dumbness. The chart below shows our current status.

We still have a long way to go. Those of you with sufficient intelligence are encouraged to donate your spare IQ points.*

*Note: Xerox policy prohibits employees above Grade 12 from donating more than 1 percent of their total points, as no surplus points are deemed to be available at that level.

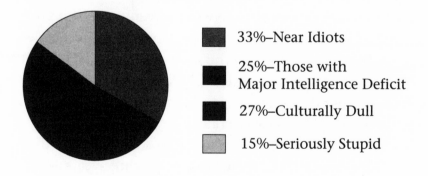

- 33%–Near Idiots
- 25%–Those with Major Intelligence Deficit
- 27%–Culturally Dull
- 15%–Seriously Stupid

Although these types of messages increase information over-load, they add interest, humanity, and humor to the work-place. This is part of the "tittle-tattle" of daily life that keeps things lively and fosters community.

The important thing is to design technology that simplifies work. At the same time, don't let old technologies hamper in-formation sharing. If your systems are not yet integrated, as-semble information manually. Many of us have done it, and though it is not easy or convenient, it's better than not shar-ing information at all. Don't let anyone postpone opening the books until the technology is perfect. You could wait till pigs fly.

The interesting thing about the convergence of open-book information with technology is that both have enormous shape-shifting potential for enterprises and society. This con-vergence will undoubtedly bring unintended consequences—possibly the kinds of upheavals that accompanied the invention of the printing press: renaissance and reformation. And it's this fear of the unknown that keeps people stuck. But what are the alternatives? Closed, hypocritical systems are counterproductive. Dishonesty breeds dishonesty; hypocrisy breeds hypocrisy.

The television news program *60 Minutes* recently did a story on a thirty-three-year-old Hollywood screenwriter who pre-tended to be nineteen in order to get work. It seems that de-spite vehement denials from the show-business establishment, Hollywood is plagued by "ageism." Many studios are run by people in their thirties, managers intent on capturing the "youth market." Writers who once wrote for TV shows like *M*A*S*H* and *All in the Family* delete those credits from their résumés because it dates them. This thirty-three-year-old fig-ured out how to play the system. Posing as a nineteen-year-old allowed her to say that she could write for the "youth market" because she was part of it. Her phone rang off the wall. She was a hot property. That is, until someone discovered that she was really thirty-three. Since then, she is a pariah. Hollywood insiders claim to be shocked by the lies this young woman told to get ahead.

In interviews with older screenwriters, *60 Minutes* explored Hollywood hiring practices and sought comments on the young woman's duplicity. The veteran writers found her behavior hilarious because they understood that she acted in response to a hypocritical system. One writer was particularly amused by the claims that Hollywood studio types were appalled by the woman's dishonesty. He commented, "How could they be shocked? These are the people who invented double bookkeeping."

Once more, our thinking creates organizational structures, and those structures create behaviors. Organizations will save tons of time and money if they quit moaning about people's behaviors and, instead, examine the structures that lead to the behaviors and the thinking that creates the structures. Open the books, create organizations of exceptional businesspeople, and enterprises will prosper beyond all dreams. As Francis Bacon reminds us, "Knowledge and human power are synonymous."

12

If It Weren't for Customers, We Could Get Something Done

Please hold, your call is important to us.

This call may be monitored for quality assurance.

We apologize for this delay. Please hold and someone will be with you shortly.

Due to heavy call volume, all our operators are busy. Please call back later.

Thank you for your patience.

Perhaps the biggest business hypocrisy, the broadest gap between the espoused theory and theory in use, is the deification of the customer. Xerox crafted a new slogan almost every year—Customer Satisfaction, Customer Delight, Customer Excellence, Customer Intimacy, Customer First—presumably believing that new words would make it so. I particularly liked Customer Delight because it was so much fun to watch Curt Stiles try to force those words out of his mouth. His lips would curl up like he had just taken a big swig of castor oil.

One Xerox bigwig inadvertently revealed his attitude toward customers during a videotaped interview. He proclaimed that the company would take new innovations "all the way down to the customer." The sad thing was that most folks didn't even hear the dissonance.

Automated phone systems and answering machines are but the latest customer insult. Customers feel so cared for as they dutifully press 1, then, following condescending prompts, press 2, 3, 4. . . . There is a fleeting hope that eventually a real person will come on the line. Companies apparently haven't done a cost analysis of wasted customer time. So although the espoused theory is Customer Satisfaction, the theory in use is Customer Contempt—how's that for a slogan?

One reason for these ubiquitous answering systems, besides the fact that they save a few bucks each year, is that organizations have difficulty staffing phone centers. In a recent conversation with a credit card company, I asked about the annual turnover in their call center. The manager explained that their turnover runs 40 to 50 percent annually, but he hastened to add that this was good compared with a competitor with a turnover rate of 200 percent.

Visit a call center sometime, and you'll understand why people hate working there. Enter the world of micromanagement: Individuals are continually monitored for the number of calls they make or take, the length of each call, the orders booked, or the problems solved. When you receive hang-up calls during the last days of the month, you can figure that it's call-center folks working to meet their targets. They've learned to play the system by hanging up after the phone is answered because they are monitored on the number of live customers they contact.

Call systems are a minor annoyance compared to billing systems. As much as I admire FedEx, their billing system is wretched. First of all, they bill weekly. It's like having a fervent pen pal. Then, customers are instructed to pay FedEx bills by tearing off a perforated strip along the top of the billing envelope, turning it inside out, and reusing it to return the payment. In its final form, the envelope looks like a wrinkled paper bag with ears. I tried writing "I hate your envelopes" and "These envelopes are horrible" and finally resorted to "These envelopes suck!" No response. I've written to customer service and the president—to no avail.

Most organizations are all hat and no cattle when it comes to satisfying customers. At XBS, our intent with the "We're Respondable" fable (see Chapter 10) was to raise consciousness about the individual and local behaviors that affect customer satisfaction. We knew that good customer relationships can partially compensate for dissatisfaction with impersonal billing systems and relentless collection departments. We focused on the things we could influence, having given up on the corporate types who seemed tone deaf when it came to customer needs.

It's not as if customer messages weren't reaching the organizational establishment. Paul Allaire, Xerox's CEO, tells the story of the sales rep who responded to Paul's assurance that he knew billing was a mess by saying, "No, Paul, if you really understood how bad it is, you'd do something about it." The way Xerox addressed the issue was to begin paying field people on the basis of their customer survey scores. It became the field's responsibility to make customers happy, despite lousy corporate systems. And when the field's best efforts failed, oh well, they missed a bonus. Yep, don't solve the problem. Give it to someone else. It's a great way to save compensation dollars, and to hell with customers.

Of course, this compensation solution led to other issues. People spent gobs of time arguing over the survey methodology. Here's the deal: When all else fails, argue methodology and blame someone else. Then figure out how to "game" the system.

I never uncovered the customer survey scam till I was on staff and wouldn't have played this game anyway. But I had to laugh at the scoundrels who figured out how to trick the system. Not surprisingly, Xerox billing records are rife with misspelled customer names, wrong addresses, and incorrect zip codes—and the survey system kicked back all correspondence to invalid addresses. Prior to each customer survey, the field would receive a customer list along with the request to correct spellings, addresses, and other data. In Pittsburgh we diligently scrutinized the documents, making sure the information was correct. We were such good children it was disgusting. In other places, I later learned, people intentionally input errors to guarantee that only happy customers received surveys. Then, of course, the week that the surveys were mailed, the sales reps ran around like crazy begging customers to send in good responses. The field learned to manage the survey. This is what the Institute for Research on Learning means when it says that people are learning all the time, but not always what you want them to learn.

Today, products and services are increasingly undifferentiated. Name the differences in credit card providers, airlines, outsourcing organizations, phone companies, department store chains, banks, overnight mail services. These enterprises are more alike than different.

Credit card companies entice new users with low introductory annual percentage rates, yet acknowledge that this practice leads to significant client turnover. Consumers have learned how to play this game. Many set up computer programs to track these bargain introductory periods, switching providers as soon as the cheap money runs out. Given the dollars spent on wooing new customers, wouldn't it make sense to try to hang on to them? Wouldn't it make sense to design systems and to create environments that amaze customers? In a time of undifferentiated products and services, perhaps the marketplace advantage lies in *who we are* as much as in *what we do.*

Culture and organizational structures are inextricably intertwined—and in no area is this more apparent than in customer service. When we ask people to satisfy clients yet fail to fix the systems that drive customers crazy, we create organizational schizophrenia. It's like asking someone to wallpaper a room with one hand tied behind the back. In *Toward a Theory of Schizophrenia,* Gregory Bateson refers to this condition as the "double bind" and hypothesizes that people caught in "damned if you do, damned if you don't" situations are susceptible to schizophrenic symptoms.

One reason that customer service issues are often overlooked is that they are difficult to quantify. It's hard to prove precisely how investments in customer satisfaction will enrich the bottom line. Unfortunately, our fixation on metrics creates narrow, short-term thinking. Sometimes it takes a major snafu to bring corporate types to their senses.

If you want a highly quantifiable example of how corporate structure, culture, and attitudes toward customers can lead to behaviors that affect the bottom line, look at Sears. Since 1992 and the arrival of new CEO Arthur Martinez, Sears has been engaged in major restructuring and market repositioning. In addition to abolishing the old Sears catalog and recasting Sears as a retailer of high-profit apparel lines, Martinez encouraged the expansion of Sears's credit business, extending credit cards to 17 million new customers. A 1997 *Barrons* article praised Sears's ability to trim losses by aggressively pursuing bad debts.

Just a few months before publication of the *Barrons* article and an anticipated *Fortune* feature on Sears's comeback, a retired security guard, Francis Latanowich, wrote a letter to Judge Carol Kenner at the federal bankruptcy court in Boston. He begged that his bankruptcy case be reopened because although Judge Kenner had wiped out his debts, Latanowich had agreed to repay Sears the $1,161 he owed prior to his bankruptcy, and the payments were "keeping food off the table for my kids." Although it is legal for creditors to offer bankrupt debtors the option of signing reaffirmations and accepting responsibility for old bills, reaffirmations must be filed with the court so that the judge can determine whether the debtor can handle the payments. Judge Kenner had not approved Latanowich's reaffirmation with Sears. What quickly became clear was that Sears had ignored the law, not only in this case, but in 2,733 cases in Massachusetts since 1995. Moreover, following further probing, Sears admitted that it had illegally collected $110 million from 187,000 consumers.

As soon as Martinez realized the scope of Sears's legal issues, he assembled the top two hundred company executives and sadly explained Sears's dilemma. At the end of the meeting, he asked that each person spend time thinking about what in the Sears culture caused such a thing to happen. "Is what I do, the direction I give, the body language I use, creating an environment where something like this could happen? Is my message 'Make the numbers at any cost'?"

Although Martinez had taken steps to set a tone of integrity, including the formation of an ethics office, he also initiated massive layoffs and cost cutting. Simultaneously, he pushed for growth in the credit operation, rapidly expanding the cardholder base to increasingly risky customers. By 1997, over one-third of personal bankruptcies listed Sears as a creditor.

Martinez reflected deeply on the cultural flaws that led to this scandal. "Maybe the bullshit that's being written about how we've changed values and culture is just that. What allowed this thing to go unnoticed, untouched, and unreported for so long?" he asked his executives. What Martinez and his execs concluded was that nobody wanted to be the bearer of bad news. But Martinez also commented that the reason nobody blew the whistle might have arisen from deep beliefs about customers. He said, "I'm sure our people would say, 'These goddamn deadbeats; they took the merchandise and they didn't pay for it, and they filed for bankruptcy. I'm going to find a way to protect my company.' That's wrongheaded, but it's an accurate reflection of the culture."

As Sears continued to investigate the patterns that led to these illegal activities, it became clear that a number of people had been aware of the practice yet kept quiet. Sears also discovered that its own procedure manual was ambiguous and could be construed as supporting the non-filing of reaffirmations. These discoveries solidified Sears's resolve to come clean, to pay restitution in full, and to avoid years of litigation and bad press. "We had to admit to failure here and commit to repaying people the money we'd inappropriately collected," Martinez said. "We said to ourselves, 'We can't go into court and defend any of our practices.'" Michael Levin, a Sears lawyer, encouraged the corporation to admit that its own "flawed legal judgment" was to blame for the misconduct. After a Sears subsidiary pleaded guilty to bankruptcy fraud, Sears paid the federal government's $60 million fine, the largest of its type in U.S. history.

What's admirable in this story is Sears's admission of culpability and acceptance of responsibility. This behavior sends powerful messages to people within the culture. Sears spent

$14 million searching its records for illegal reaffirmations and locating the customers owed refunds. When all is said and done, the scandal will have cost Sears almost $475 million, a number that doesn't count the costs of lowered employee morale, diminished reputation, and erosion in the stock price. Sears's turnaround has faltered in the wake of this scandal, and although Martinez has announced his "Second Revolution"—a plan that includes store remodelings and fresh product lines—it's unclear whether he'll be able to reenergize the enterprise.

Martinez was asking the right questions, recognizing that something in the organizational environment led to unethical behaviors. Something in the culture encouraged people to keep quiet about collection practices run amok. A good guess: fear. It's not surprising that the policy manual was fuzzy on the legal issues. Rules are usually written by staffers with a letter-of-the-law mentality, and in this case, the procedures that make technocrats so smug didn't help one bit. In fact, they made things worse. Policies don't lead to ethical behavior. Never did, never will.

Behaviors, values, and attitudes cannot be legislated; they cannot be trained into people or brought into existence by announcements, slogans, or videos. Behaviors arise from structures, and structures arise from thinking. Listen to discussions within organizations—conversations about compensation, about cost containment, about market coverage—and count the number of times somebody thinks to ask, "How will this affect customers?" We treat customers as afterthoughts, referring to them as "accounts," or "establishments." We are estranged from customers. We forget that customers are us.

Sears has a wonderful opportunity to become the kind of community they really want to be. If I were Sears, I'd use this scandal as the foundation for a transformation strategy—not

one characterized by slogans and rah-rah meetings. The strategy would lead to testing every assumption about "the way
things are"; it would engage every employee in conversations
about customers, the marketplace, and the future. In fact, customers, stockholders, and other stake-holders would be part of
these conversations.

The strategy would invite Sears people to codesign the future, to shape a productive, ethical community where a scandal like this could never happen again. Every person would
come to understand that Sears would thrive only if customers
are thrilled with products and services and if Sears creates an
environment that nurtures its own people. Every person
would become a marketing person, able to analyze financials
and figure out ways to enhance the bottom line. Every person
would become a co-owner of the business. As inspirational as
Martinez appears to be, he would increase his chances of success exponentially if he has 100 percent of his people helping
him create a new future for Sears. The investment? Well, it
wouldn't come close to $475 million.

It's time to call businesses on their shoddy customer service.
It's time that companies close the gap between what they say
and the way they behave. Part of the solution is systemic. We
can address the solution only by examining our collective
thinking and redesigning internal systems that nurture the behaviors and attitudes that lead to unbelievable customer service. Yet, I remain convinced that individuals within
organizations can create disturbances that influence the system at large. By creating the future now, we actualize what
these organizations can look like and feel like, and demonstrate the business results of new approaches. One way to start
is by looking for organizations that are really delivering and by
learning from them.

The net is this: A company's customers will be as happy as the company's people and suppliers are. Eric Zeller, owner of Zeller Electric in Rochester, New York, says, "If you mistreat any of these three—your customers, your people, or your suppliers—then you're through." Eric has built a highly successful organization based on this philosophy.

Zeller Electric has grown from $6 million to $30 million in revenues over the past thirteen years. The company operates on three principles:

The most important thing in your life is your personal health. You are responsible for taking care of yourself first, for eating right, sleeping enough, getting the right kind of exercise, and nurturing yourself mentally.

The second important thing is your family. Take care of your spouse, your children, your parents, and your extended family.

The third important thing is work. When the first two are taken care of, come to work.

Zeller recognizes that if people are sick or struggling with family issues, they can't be effective. But when they are encouraged to place priority on their health and personal problems, they come back to work energized. "This has been a good policy for our company," Zeller comments.

Zeller's whole organization is based on a philosophy of abundance. He believes that there is plenty of money to go around. His fifty employees share in the success of this electrical distribution business through a generous profit-sharing program. Profits have been so good that bonuses often make up 75 percent of a person's annual income, even though the compensation package is structured as a 75 percent salary, 25 percent bonus plan. Zeller shares all financial information, including his own income—which is a significant dollar amount. Nobody complains about what he makes because everyone is doing well. Last year, when the automation marketplace softened, Zeller and his people actually made 15 percent less than the year before. But because they understand the financials and marketplace dynamics, they knew this was a temporary setback and went about business as usual.

It's not surprising that Zeller has virtually no turnover. In addition to generous compensation, Zeller's pays 100 percent of health benefits, contributes 10 percent of annual salaries to the retirement plan, and puts $500 per year per employee toward life insurance. New employees get two weeks of vacation, and by the time they've worked there eight years, they get a month. And twice a month, people can unwind with a free massage from a physical therapist who visits the office.

The company has a catered lunch every day—worth $1,200 per person per year. When this was mentioned in the local newspaper, Zeller got a phone call from a customer saying that he didn't want to pay for this kind of perk. Eric's reply: "Listen, I'm here to keep my people happy, not to pay money to the IRS. These lunches cost five hundred dollars per person per year, although, if purchased at restaurants, they would cost at least twelve hundred. And if I raised salaries by twelve hundred dollars a year, then people would just have to pay part of it in taxes. Besides, I notice that you help yourself to lunch every time you're here."

Zeller notes that because the business is so fast-paced, it is critical that people are intellectually stimulated and open to new thinking and fresh ideas. "We all have to constantly expand our minds and look at the world differently," he says. He insists that each person take five days a year for self-education. People can sign up for anything, and although some take work-related courses, many don't. He told me about one person who recently took a wine-tasting seminar. "Yes, we paid for her to go drink wine. All she had to do was to share her learning with everyone else when she got back."

Furthermore, there are no rules about who can spend how much money. Anyone can spend whatever is needed to get the job done. Eric told me the story of an employee who went out and bought a five-thousand-dollar motor to use in a customer demonstration. It was the only way he could exhibit the solution he was proposing to the customer. The customer was duly impressed, and Zeller expects to get this customer's business. Eric says that every time he sees that motor, he laughs. Another person recently spent two thousand dollars on a new piece of equipment that will make it easier to do his job. When the guy explained why he made the purchase, Eric laughed and said, "Well, bless you, I hope it works."

Zeller's customers are delighted. Although the company conducts annual customer surveys, they also look for ways to get timely customer feedback. Recently, every person in the company talked to six customers over a two-week period, asking just a few simple questions and soliciting input for how Zeller could improve customer service. They got four or five pretty good ideas and implemented them immediately. Zeller comments, "We'll try anything. We just experiment and see what works."

Zeller Electric's environment nurtures the people who work there. The dining room is filled with expensive artwork—something Zeller takes for granted. He comments, "People like being surrounded with beautiful things. It makes them feel good." And he's onto something. Mary Catherine Bateson notes that "objects that enrich the senses also enrich human relationships."

Zeller's only problem is growth, a very nice problem to have. He shares that at certain points, current financial systems and tracking mechanisms just won't accommodate any more data. But the organization's experimental mentality and willingness to spend the money required to support the increasing business volume ensures the company's future success. Zeller Electric has created a humane, happy workplace.

There's no gap here between what is said and what is done. This organization lives its values. People are free to experiment, free to make decisions, free to make mistakes. It's an organization based not on fear, but on love.

> To my mind there must be
> at the bottom of it all, not an equation
> but an utterly simple idea
> And to me that idea, when we
> finally discover it,
> will be so compelling, so inviolate
> that we'll say to one another
> Oh, how beautiful.
> How could it have been otherwise?
>   **John Archibald Wheeler**

13

Come Hell or High Water

Ideology is a specious way of relating to the world.

It offers human beings the illusion of an identity, of dignity, and of morality while making it easier for them to part with them.

As the repository of something suprapersonal and objective, it enables people to deceive their conscience and conceal their true position and their inglorious modus vivendi, both from the world and from themselves. . . . It is a veil behind which human beings can hide their own fallen existence, their trivialization, and their adaption to the status quo. . . . The primary excusatory function of ideology, therefore, is to provide people, both as victims and pillars of the post-totalitarian system, with the illusion that the system is in harmony with the human order and the order of the universe.

Vaclav Havel

In his essay "The Power of the Powerless," Vaclav Havel writes about how each of us creates our world. And although he described the Czechoslovakia of 1978—long before he became president of that country—some of his words evoke American institutional life.

As I consult and speak throughout the country, I am struck by the mixture of anger and sadness that arises when people talk about their workplaces. They describe their institutions as hollow, dehumanizing, mind-numbing, and dishonest; many see themselves as powerless. In a recent working session with sixty-five highly educated and well-paid professionals, one participant drew a picture of how the group looked within the organizational context. She sketched an inverted triangle intersected with many layers. Near the bottom of the triangle, she drew a tiny square. The layered triangle represented the institution; the tiny square signified this group of professionals. It was surprising because, relatively, these people are well respected and influential, but, in fact, they no longer view themselves that way. They feel oppressed, unappreciated, and frustrated. The enemy is out there, up there, over there—anywhere but here. They have been sucked into the institutional undertow and are struggling to understand that some of their own behaviors perpetuate the very conditions they deplore.

Havel tells the story of the grocer who places a sign in his window that says, "Workers of the world, unite!" The sign has been shipped to him from enterprise headquarters along with vegetables, fruits, and other foodstuffs. He put it in the window, not because it represented his views, but because everybody had been doing it for years. He didn't do it to acquaint passers-by with the sentiment expressed. He did it without thought.

The slogan is really a sign, and as such it contains a subliminal but very definite message. Verbally, it might be expressed this way: "I, the greengrocer XY, live here and I know what I must do. I behave in the manner expected of me. I can be depended upon and am beyond reproach. I am obedient and therefore I have the right to be left in peace." . . . If the greengrocer had been instructed to display the slogan "I am afraid and therefore unquestioningly obedient," he would not have been nearly as indifferent to its semantics, even though it would reflect the truth.

The rituals, customs, and ideologies of organizations have similar effects on the humans living within them. Many of us do things because they are habitual and expected. We don't question or challenge. We give up power. We surrender to the status quo and become unthinking, obedient drudges.

There is no question that structures, practices, and culture affect how people think and behave. An interesting experiment conducted at Stanford back in the seventies illuminates the way structures affect the people living within them. Researchers wanted to understand the behaviors and attitudes of both prisoners and guards within penal institutions. They constructed a simulated prison environment; they selected a group of twenty-two volunteers who were homogeneous— Caucasian and middle class. None of the volunteers knew each other at the start of the project.

Although participants were subjected to a battery of psychological tests, the experimenter-observers did not analyze this data prior to the experiment, to avoid biasing themselves. The subjects were briefed on the nature of the experiment and told that they would be randomly assigned roles of prisoner or guards.

The participants selected as guards were oriented and given minimal guidelines except to "maintain the reasonable degree of order within the prison necessary for its effective functioning." They were prohibited, however, from using physical punishment or physical aggression. The guards became involved in the experiment before the induction of the prisoners, helping to set up the cells and complete the guard quarters.

Both the prisoners and the guards were assigned uniforms, which enhanced group identity and reduced individuality within the two groups. The guards wore militaristic khaki uniforms and carried whistles and nightsticks as symbols of their control and power. The prisoners' uniforms—ankle chains that continually reminded them of the oppressive environment, stocking caps that removed the distinctiveness associated with hair color and style, and loose, ill-fitting, dresslike clothing worn without underwear—served to emasculate and rob the subjects of their individual identities.

Although the subjects were free to interact in any way they chose, those playing prisoners became passive, withdrawn, and depressed while those playing guards became assertive and forceful. Five prisoners became so enraged and anxious that they had to be released early from the study. Although some guards were noncoercive with prisoners and some stuck to the guidelines defined at the beginning of the experiment, others became abusive, hostile, and overbearing, stripping prisoners of their rights and, in one case, holding a prisoner in solitary confinement while attempting to conceal this information from the researchers, who were seen as being too easy on the prisoners.

The guards' aggression escalated daily. One was observed pacing, "vigorously pounding his nightstick into his hand while he 'kept watch' over his captives. . . . After the first day of the study, practically all prisoner rights (even such things as the time and conditions of sleeping and eating) came to be redefined by the guards as 'privileges' which were to be earned by obedient behavior. . . . 'Reward' then became granting approval for prisoners to eat, sleep, go to the toilet, talk, smoke a cigarette, wear eyeglasses, or the temporary diminution of harassment." Even the "good" guards who didn't participate in abusive behavior did nothing to interfere with their hostile peers.

What was clear from observation and from postexperiment interviews was that power was exhilarating, self-aggrandizing, and self-perpetuating. When the researchers called off the experiment after only six days, the remaining prisoners were thrilled, whereas most guards were distressed. "They had become sufficiently involved in their roles that they now enjoyed the extreme control and power which they exercised and were reluctant to give it up."

This study offers interesting insight into the pathology of power and dependency. Although the prisoners initially protested their treatment with rebellion and later set up a grievance committee, when they met with no success their group cohesion disintegrated and they turned on each other. Some became sick; others became excessively obedient, siding with guards against fellow prisoners. The prisoners' self-regard was the product of believing that the hostility toward them was justified. As the experiment continued, the model prisoners became ever more passive and dependent. The experimenters attributed these reactions to loss of personal identity, to the arbitrary controls, "capricious decisions and rules of the guards," and to the dependency and emasculation experienced in their prisoner roles.

Although I'm not suggesting that organizations are prisons, structures do influence how people behave. Institutional systems, with their tacit demand for conformity and a plethora of arbitrary rules, sometimes have the effect of paralyzing people, of blinding them to what is really going on. What's interesting about the experiment is that the "good" guards did not protest as more aggressive guards abused prisoners. This mirrors behaviors often observed within organizations. People complain about inequities but keep their views private, allowing unethical and unfair practices to continue. This has got to stop.

Humans have created organizational structures; humans therefore can rethink and redesign them. And the impetus for change will come when people refuse to go along with destructive rules and unfair practices. It's always interesting to see how dissent arises because it often happens indirectly, in very unexpected ways, around issues seemingly peripheral to matters at hand. Havel explains that in Czechoslovakia, for instance, the incident that led to the appearance of Charter 77, a demand that governmental practices be consistent with government's own laws, was the 1976 trial of two obscure rock groups. The government put the musicians on trial because rock music was officially forbidden as it was seen as a threat to the totalitarian regime.

> In some ways the trial was the final straw. Many groups of differing tendencies which until then had remained isolated from each other, reluctant to cooperate, or which were committed to forms of action that made cooperation difficult, were suddenly struck with the powerful realization that freedom is indivisible. Everyone understood that an attack on the Czech musical underground was an attack on a most elementary and important thing, something that in fact bound everyone together: it was an attack on the very notion of living within truth, on the real aims of life. The freedom to play rock music was understood as a human freedom and thus as essentially the same as the freedom to engage in philosophical and political reflection, the freedom to write, the freedom to express and defend the various social and political interests of society. People were in-

spired to feel a genuine sense of solidarity with the young musicians
and they came to realize that not standing up for the freedom of
others, regardless of how remote their means of creativity or their
attitude to life, meant surrendering one's own freedom.

Intellectuals, artists, activists, and other ordinary humans
living within the Soviet bloc had a choice: They could comply
with the repressive strictures of a despotic system, or they
could choose to live within truth. The people who opted to
live within truth rather than support an artificial world of appearances did so out of the recurring realization that totalitarian systems were at odds with life. As Havel says, "While life,
in its essence, moves toward diversity, independent self-consti-
tution, and self-organization, in short, toward the fulfillment
of its own freedom, the post-totalitarian system demands conformity, uniformity, and discipline."

What had emerged over a period of years was a vibrant underground community of people who demonstrated that "living in truth is a human and social alternative." This group did
not set out to overthrow the government. They began living as
they saw fit, creating what Havel describes as "the independent life of society," a second culture. "These parallel structures, it may be said, represent the most articulated
expressions so far of living within truth."

Eventually, of course, this underground created the social
ferment that erupted with the trial of the rock musicians.
What the supporters of Charter 77 ("Chartists") did was elegant in its simplicity. They publicly proclaimed what was obvious to all citizens. Although the government espoused its
support for the rights of all people, laws were ignored or dis-
honored when it was in the government's interest to do so.
The Chartists merely pointed out the gap between the es-

poused theory and the theory in use and demanded that the government adhere to laws derived from the constitution and the international agreements ratified by the regime.

In his essay "Chartism and 'Real Socialism,'" Moroslav Kusy explains the paradox that the regime faced with Charter 77:

> The Charter openly criticizes the reality of real socialism by holding up the moral and political principles publicly acknowledged by the regime itself, by demanding that the regime practice what it preaches. Truth and justice are not Charter inventions but ancient moral values and political principles that even the communist movement has emblazoned on its escutcheon. It is in their name that real socialism operates. Such a regime, therefore, cannot oppose the Charter frontally. It cannot publish the Charter and its documents, refute its arguments; it cannot harass and lock up Chartists openly for their association with the Charter. The strength of this political aspect of the Charter leads to a paradoxical reversal of roles; the powerless Charter appeals to the law while the legitimate regime struggles against it using Mafia techniques, by breaking and abusing the law.

Although the government began instituting reforms, making half-baked efforts to integrate the values of this social underground into official policy, Havel and his colleagues recognized that these attempts to appropriate liberal ideas without fundamentally altering command-and-control structures were ways of muddying the line between living within truth and living with a lie. They noted the differences between the values and beliefs of the underground and the government's diluted attempts at compromise.

Although the social ferment that erupted in Czechoslovakia in 1976 did not lead to an immediate redesign of government structures, it shifted the societal mood and changed the way

power was exercised. We know now that it was one of the disturbances that led to the revitalization of life within that re-
gion. Havel points out that people began living within truth,
not to overthrow the regime, but because taking this stance
had broad implications. "Historical experience teaches us that
any genuinely meaningful point of departure in an individual's life usually has an element of universality about it. In
other words, it is not something partial, accessible only to a restricted community, and not transferable to any other. On the
contrary, it must be potentially available to everyone; it must
foreshadow a general solution and, thus, it is not just the expression of an introverted, self-contained responsibility that
individuals have to and for themselves alone, but responsibility to and for the world."

Havel and a large community of underground dissidents influenced society by concentrating on making life better for
themselves and others in the here and now. They disturbed
the system by refusing to play along with the official structure,
by living within truth, and by doing what they could in the
present moment. Thoreau talks about the present moment in
Walden:

> In any weather, at any hour of the day or night, I have been anx-
> ious to improve the nick of time, and notch it on my stick too; to
> stand on the meeting of two eternities, the past and the future,
> which is precisely the present moment; to toe that line. You will
> pardon some obscurities, for there are more secrets in my trade than
> in most men's, and yet not voluntarily kept, but inseparable from
> its very nature. I would gladly tell all that I know about it, and
> never paint "No Admittance" on my gate.

Every day, we all stand on the meeting of two eternities. We
exist in the now. We can influence and change our communi-

ties by living within truth, by refusing to go along with practices and rituals incongruent with life, by creating environments that nurture humans, by welcoming others into our communities, by never painting "No Admittance" on our gates. Organizational and societal shifts will happen through our doing what we can, influencing the practices and rituals of our institutions along the way. Over time, disturbances have cumulative effects.

Communities of practice are the organizational equivalent of the parallel societal structures that emerged in Czechoslovakia—because communities of practice are, by their very nature, self-organizing and self-governing groups that act without formal blessing.

The unrest and dissatisfaction expressed by people within institutions arises—as it did in Czechoslovakia—from recognition that most current organizational systems are incongruent with life. It's becoming increasingly obvious that fundamental change will emerge from an invisible subculture that is developing in many enterprises. *Fast Company*'s Real Time conferences have spawned communities of practice that span organizational boundaries. Most major cities have a Company of Friends, people who subscribe to *Fast Company*'s philosophy and are looking for ways to do things differently—starting here and now. There are other coalitions influencing how institutions operate: corporate, research, and consultant members in the Society for Organizational Learning; interdisciplinary collaborators at the Santa Fe Institute; participants in the Global Business Network; Dee Hock and his Chaordic Alliance; environmentalists; activists in the ethical investment community—just to name a few.

There are many ways to influence new practices, both individually and collectively. Not long ago, I talked to a human resources professional who was entangled in her company's most recent downsizing effort. She had long been uncomfortable with how people were treated when they were laid off. They were assembled and informed that they were losing their jobs. Then they were escorted to their desks, directed to gather their personal belongings, and hustled out the door. People who had loyally served the company—sometimes for years—were treated like criminals. The entire process was degrading and dehumanizing for all concerned.

The woman went to the president of the organization and convinced him that this was a horrible way of handling an already-bad situation. The company changed its process. The scope of the downsizing effort was fully communicated up front. Everyone involved knew who was being laid off and the date of each termination. People were privy to all company information, to their computers, and to strategic plans until their actual departure. There were even farewell receptions. The organization worked from the assumption that people were trustworthy and would do the right thing. They did everything possible to treat employees with the utmost dignity and respect. And contrary to the dire predictions of downsizing specialists, the organization's people lived up to the trust the company had in them.

One person, the aforementioned human resources professional, recognized an inhumane practice and took it upon herself to make things better. Her action influenced the thinking of everyone in the system—from the people laid off to those who remained. This person saw a better way. She has shifted organizational beliefs and assumptions through doing something different in the here and now.

A large transnational firm continued to do a thriving and profitable business with the apartheid South African government long after most corporations had pulled out. This organization was eventually shamed into leaving that country by its own employees, who spoke up and wrote letters till its management took notice. The protesters were not personally affected by what was going on in South Africa; they were morally offended. They took action for the greater good.

People who become activists—whether in the domain of politics, the environment, or business—usually hold deep convictions. Most get involved because they believe in social justice and want to make things better for humans everywhere. Corporations are among the most powerful entities in the world today, woven inextricably into the social web. Change within organizations has the potential to change society and the world.

People often ask, "How can I convince my own institution that we need to change?" The short answer is that you can't. It's less direct than that, but it starts with you. First of all, it's important to decide whether you really want to be an agent of change. It's not for everyone. Thoreau likened civil disobedience to living a deliberative life. Change agents make a choice to be self-aware, self-critical, and self-examining, to lay themselves on the line. Our own immersion in these systems sometimes makes it difficult to see what's before our eyes. Change agents have to continually ask themselves, "Do I see what I believe, or do I believe what I see?"

Change agents must be prepared for skepticism and criticism of data, beliefs, methods, and motives. Havel speaks to the matter this way: "By the way, the representatives of power invariably come to terms with those who live within truth by persistently ascribing utilitarian motivations to them—a lust for power or fame or wealth—and thus they try, at least, to implicate them in their own world, the world of general demoralization."

The way to start is by beginning to live within truth, by refusing to be part of practices that are inauthentic, hypocritical, unethical, or inhumane. It's not necessary to be strident or unpleasant. But it is critical to tell the truth as you see it. At the same time, you must remain open, testing your own assumptions and beliefs at every opportunity.

Change agents must be willing to experiment, to do things differently. Whether you begin by using fresh learning methods, by acknowledging the generative power of language and selecting new words to use, or by sharing information more openly with colleagues, it's important to start doing something that creates the future now, something that begins to close the gap between the espoused theory and the theory in use.

At some point you'll be asked to explain your approaches. Make your logic explicit. Detail what you think, why you think it, and how your methods are creating more effective and productive outcomes for your enterprise. If you want to cite research, be sure to use multiple sources. I used to lay out research in grids just so I could explain it. Although the information was far more useful to me than to anyone else—because the learning came from putting the information together—the data demonstrated that my ideas weren't coming out of thin air.

Create parallel structures, a second culture. Find other people interested in doing things differently. Exchange ideas and support each other. Remain open to the notion that people interested in new approaches exist in all parts of the community—from the CEO's office to the shop floor. Inquisitive, curious, and open-minded people are everywhere. They are the ones willing to try anything new that seems to make sense. They aren't afraid of making mistakes.

Be patient. Sometimes the people who are initially resistant to new approaches accept fresh ideas over time. It's important to start where people are and to understand that learning is a process. People who seem critical and ask a lot of questions may just be trying to understand.

In *Summer Meditations,* Havel writes: "So anyone who claims that I am a dreamer who expects to transform hell into heaven is wrong. I have few illusions. But I feel a responsibility to work towards the things I consider good and right. I don't know whether I'll be able to change certain things for the better, or not at all. Both outcomes are possible. There is only one thing I will not concede: that it might be meaningless to strive in a good cause."

14

For We Are
Such Stuff

For we are such stuff as dreams are made on
And our little lives are rounded with a sleep.
William Shakespeare

As I'm sure you've guessed by now, I'm a born agitator. I've often found myself in situations not to my liking and have discovered that it doesn't pay to spend time howling at the moon. The only way to make a difference in this world is to question, to understand, and then to take action. So far, I've talked about how we can collectively change institutions to create more productive and more fulfilling workplaces. At the same time, it's vital to understand how corporations play in the societal context and the actions each of us can take to ensure that our institutions serve society as a whole.

Thanks to the U.S. government, corporations are the most powerful entities in the world today. Mark Twain said, "There is no distinctly native American criminal class except Congress." These days, the criminal class of the United States is owned by corporations—lock, stock, and barrel.

Between 1987 and 1996, Fortune 500 companies "contributed at least $182 million to members of Congress through their political action committees. 'Soft money' contributions to both parties during the same period totaled more than $73 million." These numbers, quoted in Charles Lewis's *Buying of the Congress,* are the tip of the iceberg. Buckets of money are funneled to politicians through professional associations, fund-raising events, and deep-pocketed donors. Corporations also routinely hand out all-expense-paid trips to lawmakers and jobs to congressional relatives, former officeholders, and Hill staffers.

With this kind of clout, corporations don't just get into the game; they decide what game to play, where to play it, and what the rules will be. You may be saying, "So what? I work for a corporation and I'm doing OK. Why should I care?" Look at your children. That's why you should care. What is happening in the marketplace, in corporations, and on Capitol Hill has long-term implications for us all.

When making decisions, the Iroquois think seven generations out. How will today's actions affect the next seven generations? Most of us, on the other hand, think in terms of seven days or seven months. Either we'll learn the art of the long view, or we'll put our children's futures at risk.

According to a November 9, 1998, *Time* article, the federal government shells out $125 billion a year in corporate welfare in the form of tax breaks, subsidies, funding for advertising, training, research, and the construction of plants, offices, and stores. "The justification of much of this welfare is that the U.S. government is creating jobs. Over the past six years, Congress appropriated $5 billion to run the Export-Import Bank of the United States which subsidizes companies that sell goods abroad." Although bank officers claim that U.S. workers have higher-quality jobs, thanks to the bank's financing, "the numbers at the bank's five biggest beneficiaries—AT&T, Bechtel, Boeing, General Electric and McDonald Douglas (now part of Boeing)—tell another story. At these companies, which have accounted for about 40% of all loans, grants and long-term guarantees in this decade, overall employment has fallen 38%."

Time also exposes the lunacy of state and local government giveaways, admitting that there is no accurate way to determine the amount of money that states hand over:

> That's because few want you to know. Some say they maintain no records. Some say they don't know where the files are. Some say the information is not public. All that's certain is that the figure is in the many billions of dollars each year and it is growing, when measured against the subsidy per job.
>
> And what are the costs? The equivalent of nearly two weekly paychecks from every working man and woman in America—extra money that would stay in their pockets if it didn't go to support some business venture or another.

The greater cost is to children, because in some instances communities use moneys slated for school improvements to entice corporations to the area.

So why does corporate welfare continue—even as politicians decry the evil welfare mothers, whose take is a drop in the bucket? Corporate handouts continue because an entire bureaucracy has sprung up to expand corporate welfare—an estimated eleven thousand organizations and agencies with political access. Of course, in all their seminars, newsletters, journals, they never call it welfare. They call it "economic incentives" or "empowerment zones" or "enterprise zones."

More weasel words. *Time*'s story points out the inherent unfairness of the corporate welfare system. "It tilts the playing field in favor of the largest or the most politically influential or most aggressive businesses." The article also details the millions of government dollars raked in by its own parent company, Time Warner.

The $125 billion in annual corporate welfare doled out in the United States is equivalent to all the income tax paid by 60 million individuals and families. And to add insult to injury, corporate income tax rates have fallen drastically over the past forty years. In the 1950s, corporate taxes amounted to 39 percent of federal tax revenues. From 1990 to 1995, corporate contributions made up only 19 percent of the federal income tax base, whereas revenues coming from individuals climbed to 81 percent of the total. If, in 1996, corporations had been taxed at the same effective rate as during the 1950s, the additional $250 billion in contributions would have wiped out the federal deficit for that year.

At the same time that Congress has taken care of corporations, it has also catered to its wealthy patrons, reducing income tax rates and capital gains taxes even as income within the top 1 percent of earners soared—doubling in real terms between 1977 and 1989. As Charles Lewis points out, "The United States now has the widest gap between rich and poor of any industrialized country." Moving that to the corporate sphere, in 1996, CEO pay increased 56 percent, compared with the 3 percent enjoyed by everyone else. A *Business Week* article published May 12, 1997, features former Heinz CEO Tony O'Reilly, who pocketed $64.2 million while his company trailed competitors in earnings and market value; Michael Ovitz's $91 million severance package from Disney; and Disney's CEO Michael Eisner's simultaneous reward of eight million stock options. The story says that even CEOs are squeamish about their skyrocketing earnings, acknowledging that pay has no real relation to performance, revenues, or stockholder value. So far, however, nobody has volunteered to return the dough. Proposals to cap what corporations write off for executive perks have been soundly defeated—surprise, surprise. Lawmakers aren't going to bite the hands that feed them.

In a March 1997 *Forbes* article, Peter Drucker notes, "Few top executives can even imagine the hatred, contempt and fury that has been created, not primarily among blue-collar workers who never had an exalted opinion of the 'bosses'—but among their middle management and professional people. I don't know what form it will take, but the envy developing from their enormous wealth will cause trouble."

Lou Gerstner, who axed two hundred thousand, IBM employees in 1993 and 1994, simultaneously tripled his own pay. His 1994 take—salary, bonus, and "other compensation"—was $12 million. His *let-them-eat-cake* behavior extended to flying around the country on one of the company's nine private jets and plunking down $250,000 for a float in the Rose Bowl Parade. But, after all, he did finally make some cuts in the executive suites. Yeah, he cut the secretaries' pay—probably to fund the $118,000-a-year gourmet chef for the executive dining room. What a guy.

Gerstner is by no means the only bandit riding the corporate range. Robert Allen, who slashed forty thousand AT&T jobs in 1996, took home $8 million that year, a nifty 45 percent increase over his 1995 earnings. In a *Newsweek* interview, reporter Alan Sloan confronted Allen about this greed run amok, asking the CEO whether he considered his own compensation "fair" when forty thousand other AT&T folks had lost their jobs. "Is it fair?" he replied. "Hell, I don't know. I don't make the rules."

Even as corporate officers line their own pockets, they're making arrangements to rape and pillage under the guise of "globalization." Trade agreements like GATT (General Agreement on Tariffs and Trade), NAFTA (North American Free Trade Agreement), and now the WTO (World Trade Organization) allow corporations to operate outside the law. In *There's Nothing in the Middle of the Road but Yellow Stripes and Dead Armadillos,* Jim Hightower explains:

> Technically, the WTO is the creation of governments, including ours, but in fact it is the baby of the world's corporate and financial giants— such names as GM [General Motors], Chase Manhattan, Nestlé, Caterpillar, Credit Suisse, ADM [Archer Daniels Midland], Kodak, Nippon, Goldman Sachs, GE [General Electric], Boeing, Unilever, Exxon, Monsanto, British Petroleum, and, well, the full club of powerhouse corporations that now call themselves "transnational."

Hightower cites examples of corporations riding roughshod over federal, state, and local governments, including a recent case in Massachusetts.

> Sony, Toyota, Mitsubishi, and other transnationals are presently pursuing just such an action through the World Trade Organization against the state of Massachusetts, which passed a law in 1997 saying state agencies there will not buy products from companies that do business with the brutally repressive dictatorial gangsters now ruling Burma. The corporations say uh-uh—their global trade rights supersede the legislative autonomy of the Massachusetts people. The case is pending before a WTO tribunal of faceless officials in Geneva. Their proceedings are not open to the public or the press; a state has no standing under WTO

rules so Massachusetts cannot present its own case or even be present; and there is no appeal of the tribunal's ruling.

Under the auspices of NAFTA, corporations are moving manufacturing operations to Mexico, where workers get a dollar an hour plus lunch—usually a breakfast taco. Don't get too excited that the honchos are providing food. That's just to stave off people's hunger so they can work harder. Corporations like Alcoa, Toshiba, General Electric, Ford, Johnson & Johnson, Lucent Technologies, and Bausch and Lomb rationalize poverty-level pay by pointing out that their wages are competitive with what other companies in the area are paying and are above the minimum wage set by the Mexican government. Human rights groups are beginning to raise a ruckus about corporate exploitation. One such group recently insisted that Alcoa's CEO, Paul O'Neill, visit his Mexican manufacturing plants and talk with Alcoa employees there. O'Neill discovered that minimum wage was actually sub-minimum—below what made subsistence possible. He also found health and safety violations in Alcoa plants. After firing the human resources manager, O'Neill raised wages and put soap and toilet paper in plant bathrooms—all because he came down from his ivory tower and understood the human implications of Alcoa policies. Mexican workers still don't take home the pay of their U.S. counterparts, but it's a beginning.

Another hopeful sign is that a few politicians are wising up to corporate duplicity. Jim Hightower describes a trip he took with Representative John Lewis of Atlanta, Representative David Bonoir of Michigan, and several other lawmakers to talk to citizens and to get a real sense of what was happening in the workplace. The group interviewed Anna Harris, formerly of Lucent Technologies. Harris had worked for Lucent for twenty-five years and, by the early 1990s, was making $31,000 a year just as Lucent began making noises about moving to Mexico. Under pressure from the company, Harris and others took pay cuts—in Harris's case, $5,000 a year. "I'm a single parent. I took a cut in pay to keep my job," Harris told the lawmakers. But even this concession failed to sate Lucent's greed. Shortly after NAFTA became law, Lucent closed the Atlanta plant and moved operations to Reynosa, Mexico, paying workers $1 an hour—with no benefits, of course. Harris now works part-time at a Target store for $7.50 an hour selling, among other things, the phones she once made. When asked whether phone prices had gone down as a result of Lucent's move to Mexico, Harris's eyes turned steely cold. "There's no difference in price," she said. "They're selling them for eighty to ninety dollars."

Another disturbing treaty-related development is the Intellectual Property Rights law defined by GATT and WTO. In *Biopiracy,* Vandana Shiva explains: "The TRIPs treaty of the Final Act of GATT is based on a highly restricted concept of innovation. By definition it is weighted in favor of transnational corporations, and against citizens in general and Third World peasants and forest dwellers in particular."

Shiva goes on to explain how multinationals are exploiting the creativity of indigenous people who, over centuries, have developed herbal treatments for disease and ecologically sound agricultural methods including pest-resistant crops. Corporations are racing to patent native crops and herbal cures, then hybridizing the seeds so that they will not reproduce. Corporate pirates then turn around and insist that the very villagers who developed the patented technologies pony up bucks for new seeds. Intellectual property rights have become just another commodity for greedy corporations to exploit, according to Shiva:

> The TRIPs treaty in GATT recognizes Intellectual Property Rights only as private, not common rights. This excludes all kinds of knowledge, ideas, and innovations that take place in the intellectual commons—in villages among farmers, in forests among tribespeople, and even in universities among scientists. . . . IPRs are recognized only when knowledge and innovation generate profits, not when they meet social needs. Profits and capital accumulation are the only ends to which creativity is put; the social good is no longer recognized. . . . The GATT is the platform where the capitalistic, patriarchal notion of freedom as the unrestrained right of men with economic power to own, control, and destroy life is articulated as free trade.

In *The Ethical Imperative*, John Dalla Costa documents sleazy business practices, offering evidence that in the last ten years, roughly two-thirds of U.S. corporations have been involved, to varying degrees, in some illegal behaviors:

> GM lost a class action suit from drivers hurt or killed in pickup trucks that were designed with a vulnerable side-saddle gas tank. It was also the victim of shady ethics when NBC's *Dateline* news-magazine staged an impact of the truck but used explosive charges to ignite the ruptured fuel tank. Ford carries the stigma of knowingly selling the faulty and lethal Pinto; Exxon has the stain of the *Valdez* disaster in Alaska; Wal-Mart bruised its reputation by procuring clothes for its Kathie Lee Gifford label from sweatshops; General Electric repeatedly paid fines for fraudulent billing practices and bribery scandals in its jet engine division, and, in 1993 was fined $350 million for fraud in its (since sold) Kidder Peabody unit; and AT&T's chairman, Robert Allen, became the

poster-boy for reaping millions of dollars in wealth from stock apprecia-
tion related to firing forty thousand workers—many of whom lost their
jobs for strategic failures for which Allen was responsible.

I could go on and on, but you get the drift. Corporations
have way too much power, and they're abusing it like crazy. By
buying Congress, penning new international trade laws, in-
voking Adam Smith's invisible hand to justify marketplace
plunder, and cloaking all actions in what John Ralston Saul
calls "the rhetoric, propaganda, and dialects of corporatism,"
corporate riffraff are having a field day. This is the most sophisticated kind of hocus-pocus, and we've got to put a stop to
it. Corporations were originally chartered to serve society—not
the other way around. The Constitution makes no mention of
corporations because the framers were decidedly anticorpo-
rate. Only forty corporations operated in the United States at
that time, and their actions were strictly controlled. Since
then, most corporate law has evolved through the courts.
Many of today's issues can be traced back to the 1886 case
Santa Clara County v. Southern Pacific Railroad. In this case, the
Supreme Court ruled that a corporation is a person and enti-
tled to the same legal rights and protections afforded to individuals. Since this ruling, courts have moved consistently
toward expanding corporate rights and the autonomy of corporate management. David Korten, in *The Post-Corporate
World,* puts it this way:

> Corporations now enjoy unlimited life; virtual freedom of movement
> anywhere on the globe; control of the mass media; the ability to amass
> legions of lawyers and public relations specialists in support of their
> cause; and freedom from liability for the misdeeds of wholly owned

subsidiaries. They also enjoy the presumed right to amass property and financial resources without limit; engage in any legal activity; bring liability suits against private citizens or civic organizations that challenge them; make contributions to individual candidates, political parties, and political action committees and deduct those contributions from taxable income as business expenses; withhold potentially damaging information from customers; and avoid restrictions on the advertising of harmful but legal products in the name of commercial free speech.
. . . Step-by-step, largely through judge-made law, corporations have become far more powerful than ever intended by the people and governments that created them.

The Soviet Union disintegrated because its people ceased to believe in the government's ideology. Corporations, the government, the monetary system, the laws of the land all exist because we subscribe to their legitimacy; if we don't like things the way they are, we need to kick up dust. Now, more than ever, people are seriously questioning the motives and the tactics of both business and government. Ralph Nader, the omnipresent institutional watchdog, is being joined by organizations like the Center for Public Integrity, the Center for Responsive Politics, the International Center for Ethics in Business, and the Parliament of World Religions. Human rights and environmental organizations also are ever-attentive to institutional practices. But the efforts of these groups don't take away our personal responsibility for action; each of us must decide how and when to get involved in creating a society that is good for us, our families, and the community at large.

One obvious area of opportunity is campaign finance reform—but not the watered-down versions being touted by political opportunists with their suspect rhetoric. Most current proposals are shot through with loopholes that you could drive a truck through. Campaigns should be funded from the tax base. Where would the money come from? From increased corporate taxes. No, it will not hurt the bottom line, because additional taxes will be offset by all those political contributions that corporations will no longer be allowed to make. Since lawmakers and corporations will fight campaign finance reform tooth and nail, we're really going to have to get obnoxious—making phone calls, writing letters, forming citizens caucuses, supporting the efforts of watchdog groups. Most current officeholders aren't bad people—although it's good to remind ourselves that although the median income of Americans has risen only slightly in the last twenty years, members of Congress have awarded themselves a 50 percent increase in pay over the same period. Setting that aside, lawmakers are caught up in an insidious system, and we're going to have to fight like hell to extricate them from this mess.

One thing we've all got to do is to vote. Voting rates continue to plummet. According to the Associated Press, fewer than half the electorate voted in the 1996 presidential election; off-year, state, and local races draw even lower turnout. It's vital that we become well-informed activists.

Cornel West and Roberto Mangabeira Unger outline an interesting proposal in their recent book, *The Future of American Progressivism*. They suggest that like many contemporary democracies, the United States make voting mandatory, with a fine for the violation of duty. People could abstain from voting, but only after they enter the voting booth. This is an intriguing notion on many levels. First, it would counter voter apathy and create the kind of nation that its citizens say the United States is—one in which everyone has a voice. Second, mandatory voting would force politicians to listen to all of their constituents. Currently, sophisticated polling techniques and precise demographic data enable politicians to identify likely voters and to tailor messages specifically for that population. Lawmakers will howl at the mere suggestion of mandatory voting. Soothsayers will allude to Big Brother, Big Government, Big Costs. Ignore them. Moneys needed to support mandatory voting won't hold a candle to what's being spent on corporate welfare.

And speaking of corporate welfare, we need to get rid of that, too—no matter what it's called. Jim Hightower mentions that in late 1996, Treasury Secretary Robert Rubin issued an edict to Clinton administration officials, banning the use of the words "corporate welfare." "These guys are like three-year-olds who believe that if they squeeze their eyes shut real tight, we can't see them." Politicos will argue that corporate welfare creates jobs, but all research shows that assertion to be a misrepresentation. The way that the Bureau of Labor Statistics (BLS) calculates employment numbers gives voodoo a bad name. Despite all the talk about new jobs and record unemployment, if you look carefully at the statistics you find that "new jobs" are part-time, entry-level, or contractor positions and unemployment is actually higher than reported by the BLS. There's no getting away from the increasing gap between the haves and have-nots. Economists and futurists of all stripes predict that unless trends change, affluent Americans will retreat to walled communities, living as the rich do in developing countries—fenced off from the impoverished.

Another step that would rein in corporate power is Jim Hightower's proposal for a new corporate charter, one that would make board members and managers individually responsible for the actions of their institutions. Moreover, Hightower calls for a simple constitutional amendment to read, "A corporation is not a person." These efforts would clarify the purpose of corporations—that they are here to serve society and the greater good, not vice versa.

One trend that promises to put a hitch in the corporate giddy-up is the growth of a community dedicated to socially responsible investing. In 1997, $1.85 trillion in moneys from churches, universities, and individual investors were invested in mutual funds whose portfolios were limited to enterprises that make positive contributions to society. Ethical investment funds rate corporations on their environmental practices, product and safety records, employee and workplace issues, international operations and human rights, community investment and citizenship, and weapons contracting. Screening techniques are still being developed and leave a lot to be desired—particularly in the area of employee and workplace issues. Corporations are expert at making superficial bromides look like substantive measures. As a result, the investment community needs to refine screening to bring to light issues such as the increasing pay gaps, benefit inequity, and exploitation of developing countries' populations. This investment community grew from $639 billion in managed assets in 1995 to $1.85 trillion in 1997. As this industry segment grows, socially responsive investors will have more and more influence over corporate practices. Ethical funds deliver yields comparable to the growth of the market, so consider this investment alternative.

Social responsibility is neither a clear-cut nor an easy issue. Companies doing well in one area may lag in another. A case in point is Monsanto. A March 3, 1999, article in the *New York Times* describes Monsanto CEO Bob Shapiro as a visionary who has created a nonhierarchical, free-thinking, informal

workplace. The article points out that even though "some crit-
ics have dismissed Mr. Shapiro's style as New Age management," the CEO's commitment to organizational culture was
one reason that a potential merger with American Home Products collapsed. Monsanto corporate officers sit in cubes like
everyone else, and everyone is on a first-name basis. American
Home Product's culture is traditional command-and-control.
"Monsanto employees spoke up and disagreed with 'Bob'
while American Home officials deferred to 'Mr. Stafford,'" is
the way an observer described the merger deliberations. It became clear that to merge with American Home Products would
compromise the Monsanto culture.

But at the same time that Shapiro works to create a corporate
environment based on "authenticity and caring," Monsanto
has been loudly criticized for its genetic engineering practices.
In 1996 Monsanto charged U.S. farmers $51 million in tech-
nology fees to plant genetically engineered cotton that was
supposed to resist boll weevils. Unfortunately, after doling out
$51 million for "peace of mind" (Monsanto's words), the farm-
ers still had to spray their crops, which—despite Monsanto
claims—attracted bollworms in record numbers.

"Monsanto 'owns' the crop when it comes to reaping millions of dollars in rent from farmers, but it does not own the
costs or take responsibility for the hazards that its transgenic
crop creates," explains Vandana Shiva.

Biotechnology is rife with ethical questions, and many of
Monsanto's practices, including their shortage of research on
the long-term effects of genetically engineered crops, are being
scrutinized by environmental and ethical groups. The paradox
is that Shapiro's humanity appears to stop at his company's
borders. So, should socially concerned investors include Monsanto in their portfolios? Individuals and institutions have to

look at Monsanto's practices—good and bad—and decide for themselves.

Monsanto's case is typical. Most corporations regularly mix admirable deeds with shady dealings. For people who live and work within these environments, the challenge is to determine where the truth lies, because all establishments—business and government—are great at obfuscation and denial. *This is our story and we're sticking to it.* We've all got to get better at questioning official "truth" and conventional wisdom.

In discussions of campaign finance reform, for example, the Republicans and Democrats each blame the other, and the public chooses sides based on sound bites. Truth be known, both parties are complicit in this matter, so don't believe any of these partisans. Demand publicly funded campaigns for incumbents. James Carville has proposed that incumbent campaign funding be tied to dollars raised by challengers. For every dollar a challenger raises, an incumbent would receive funding for a lesser amount—perhaps eighty-five cents on the dollar. The rationale is that challengers need more money to set up fund-raising mechanisms. This proposal and others like it deserve careful consideration, and we all need to be part of that conversation.

Whether we're dealing with daily workplace issues, corporate practices, or the public domain, our approaches to creating the world we want will require intellectual rigor, ethical imagination, vigilance, and courage—or gumption, as my grandmother used to say.

Intellectual rigor is the opposite of all hat and no cattle. It requires that we open ourselves up to new perspectives, continually educate ourselves, question conventional wisdom, reject superficial explanations, become independent thinkers, and be willing to acknowledge what we don't know. It demands that we never lose what Einstein called "the holy curiosity."

One bit of conventional wisdom that bears scrutiny, for instance, is the current belief that all government entities, all utilities, all services should operate on a corporate profit-and-loss model. The background assumption seems to be that everything should be quantifiable, cost-justifiable in and of itself. We must consider whether this thinking serves us well. Let's use Amtrak as an example. We once had a first-class rail system, one that got gutted in the name of becoming "lean and mean." Amtrak is still trying to recover. When we look at enterprises on a stand-alone basis, a business model approach may make sense. But maybe railways should be considered overhead, part of our country's infrastructure. The French regard rail service as an essential public utility, continually investing in new equipment, new rail beds, and upgraded offerings. Trains are fast, clean, adequately staffed, frequent, and on time. Property values throughout France rise according to their proximity to train stations. Businesses are attracted to easily accessible provincial towns, creating jobs throughout the economy. There is a definite payoff, but it doesn't show up on the railway balance sheets. So when we hear proposals that government services be privatized, we need to question the underlying assumptions and carefully weigh the pros and cons of such approaches.

Intellectual rigor needs to be informed by ethical imagination. How will actions taken by government, by corporations, by individuals inside bureaucratic systems, and by each of us in our personal lives affect others? In his book *Free Markets and Social Justice,* Cass Sunstein emphasizes the importance of social justice within market systems:

A just society should be closely attentive to the background conditions against which markets proceed . . . markets will not promote justice unless they are made part of a system that offers minimally decent opportunities for all. In existing societies that use markets, the ideal of equal or even decent opportunities is violated on a daily basis. . . . That is hardly a reason to abandon markets. But it is a reason to insist on the priority of democratic goals, including social justice, to market ordering—while enlisting, much of the time, the latter in service of the former.

Whether we're talking about social justice in society or creating more meaningful work environments, our individual responsibility is the same—to evaluate our own actions against the background of what we know is fair and right. In *Dreamer,* a fictionalized biography of Martin Luther King, Charles Johnson expresses it this way: "The challenge of the spiritual was simply this: to be good, truly moral, and in control of oneself for this moment only, because what other moment in time could a man be held responsible for?"

Vigilance comes down to being attentive to the present moment, to noticing what is going on around us, to questioning glib assurances that all is well. The purpose of continual education is to heighten our own awareness that this is how life happens, from moment to moment, and that chance favors the prepared mind. Thinking about the problems of the world can be overwhelming. Mindfulness—being acutely aware of what's happening in the now—falls well within our circles of influence.

Intellectual rigor, ethical imagination, and vigilance help us understand actions within the social context, but actual change comes through living in truth and taking action—and action requires gumption. One person who has consistently displayed all these qualities is Nelson Mandela. Mandela first became involved in political protest against the South African government in the early forties, joining the African National Congress (ANC) in 1942. A small group of ANC activists became disgusted with the ANC's old guard, whose polite petitioning of the government showed no signs of achieving national emancipation. Mandela and other young revolutionaries were convinced that freedom could only be realized by creating a mass movement of millions of working people in the towns and countryside, rural peasants, and educated black professionals in the battle for liberation.

Mandela's involvement in defiance campaigns, organized resistance to discriminatory legislation, and strikes against the government continued even as he opened the first black law firm in South Africa. He was constantly harassed by the government, periodically jailed, and tried for treason. He went underground in the early 1960s and, through the military wing of the ANC, waged a campaign of sabotage against government and economic installations. He was jailed shortly thereafter and remained imprisoned for almost thirty years. Although he was offered his freedom several times in return for renouncing violence or leaving South Africa, Mandela refused, never wavering in his devotion to democracy, equality, and learning.

Shortly after his release in 1990, Mandela was elected president of the African National Congress and continued his fight for social justice. He accepted the 1993 Nobel Peace Prize on behalf of all South Africans who suffered and sacrificed to bring peace to that country. In 1994, he was elected president of South Africa. His is an amazing story. At every stage of his life, Mandela had the courage of his convictions and continued to live within truth, whatever the consequences. His power comes—then and now—not from his title, but from his willingness be the change he wants to see in the world. In his inauguration address, he said:

> Our deepest fear is not that we are inadequate,
> Our deepest fear is that we are powerful beyond measure.
> It is our light, not our darkness that most frightens us.
> We ask ourselves, who am I to be brilliant, gorgeous, talented, and
>   fabulous?
> Actually, who are you not to be?
> You are a child of God.
> Your playing small doesn't change the world.
> There is nothing enlightened about shrinking
> So that other people won't feel insecure around you.
> We are born to make manifest the glory
> Of God that is within us.
> It's not just in some of us. It's in everyone.
> And as we let our own light shine,
> We unconsciously give other people
> Permission to do the same.
> As we are liberated from our own fear,
> Our presence automatically liberates others.

The institutions we've created condition us to fear our own light, alienating us from the very power we possess to transform them and the world at large. Changing the world through re-creating institutions begins with an effort to embrace our own light, our own capabilities to question, to think, to disturb, and to act. By choosing to see ourselves as potentialities of change in our immediate environment, we empower ourselves to transform our social context, to change the present—the only moment we can ever be responsible for.

Afterword

The problem with finishing a book is that while writing the last line, you know—sure as shootin'—that you'll soon discover new resources and stories that enhance and clarify the content. My solution to this dilemma is to set up my Web page in a way that will allow for ongoing conversations with readers, updates on resource material, and images that can be used to share the ideas in *All Hat and No Cattle*. I'll be interested in your feedback, your experiences, and your stories, so please don't be strangers.

www.corporateoutlaw.com
cturner@frontiernet.net

From Future Never to Future Now Organizations

Future Never	Future Now
Frenetic organizations	Mindful organizations
Leaders as managers	Leaders as environmentalists
Change driven top-down	Change created organically
Change viewed as "from A to B"	Change as an ongoing condition
Focus on what we want to change	Focus on what we want to conserve
Talk about the change we want	Become the change we want
Individuals are victims of institutions	Individuals are cocreators of institutions
Problems are created by external situations	Problems are created by our own thinking
Communication is a thing	Communication is everything
Knowledge is a substance that can be placed in people's heads	Knowledge is created in the spaces between people
Change is up to others	Change is up to all of us
Change happens through official programs	Change is created moment to moment
Say one thing, do another (hypocrisy)	Weave outcomes we want into everything we do (integrity)
Words are no big deal	Words have generative power
Business is run by managers, who comprise 5 percent of the workforce	Everyone is an exceptional businessperson
Assumptions are invisible	Assumptions are visible
Mechanism	Mechanism
Rationalism	Rationalism
Puritanism	Puritanism
Patriarchy	Patriarchy
Classism	Classism
Cultural norms	Cultural norms
Worldview is closed	Worldview is open to include
My way or the highway	Diversity
(either/or)	Complexity theory
	Biological perspectives
	New ways of doing (and/also)
Organization as a collection of functions	Organization as a community
Corporations are a world unto themselves	Corporations are part of the social web
Focus on stock price and short-term results	Focus on social responsibility and long-term results
Institutions based on fear/scarcity	Institutions based on love/abundance

Bibliographical Essay

All Hat and No Cattle is not a footnote kind of book, but obviously the ideas have been fed by considerable research and the work of other writers. Although I've tried to cite sources throughout the text, I'll summarize background books and articles for readers who want to dig further. Using the principle of simultaneity, this essay weaves sources and bibliography into a single narrative.

There are several works that articulate how the linear, logical, fragmented view of life came to dominate Western thinking. *Voltaire's Bastards* by John Ralston Saul (Vintage Books, 1993) is a history of rationality and, although lengthy and dense with ideas, is highly accessible to the general reader. Saul's more recent book, *The Unconscious Civilization* (Free Press, 1995), deals with the same phenomenon that I call all hat and no cattle. In *Thought as a System* (Routledge, 1994) and *Wholeness and the Implicate Order*, David Bohm articulates his beliefs about the wholeness of reality, the intertwining of thought and matter. Despite being the most distinguished theoretical physicist of his time, Bohm writes with elegant simplicity, eschewing scientific jargon. Thomas Gilovich's *How We Know What Isn't So* (Free Press, 1991) is another wonderful resource on the fallibility of our own reasoning.

Two books that offer introductions to complexity theory and organizations as natural systems are *Complexity*, by Mitchell Waldrop (Touchstone, 1992), and Meg Wheatley's *Leadership and the New Science* (Berrett-Koehler Publishers, 1992). Waldrop weaves ideas about complex-adaptive systems into the story of the Santa Fe Institute, whereas Wheatley extends these ideas into the organizational domain. I also recommend *GAIA: A Way of Knowing*, edited by William Irwin Thompson, and *GAIA*, vol. 2, *Emergence* (Lindisfarne Press, 1987 and 1991). Both include selected readings from Lynn Margulis, Gregory Bateson, Francisco Varela, and other generative thinkers. *The Web of Life*, by Frijof Capra (Anchor/Doubleday, 1996), provides a synthesis of living systems theory and is a fun read. The story of the Valujet crash from William Langewiesche's *Inside the Sky* (Pantheon Books, 1998), cited in Chapter 1, illustrates how interactive complexity looks in everyday life and explains the phenomenon of "systems accidents," also called "normal accidents." Brian Arthur's ideas are detailed fully in *Increasing Returns and Path Dependence* (University of Michigan Press, 1998), but my quotes from Arthur, Richard Pascale, and Jim Marsh have been extracted from personal notes taken at the Santa Fe Institute.

It's difficult to find anything written on ethnography in the business setting, although underlying themes of the participant-observer approach are embedded within Mary Catherine Bateson's *Peripheral Visions: Learning Along the Way* (HarperCollins, 1994). *Grooming, Gossip, and the Evolution of Language* (Harvard University Press, 1996) also contains ideas that tie to ethnography. Most ethnographic information shared here comes from my work and continuing conversations with the field researchers from the Institute for Research on Learning and the Palo Alto Research Center. The final report for XBS, *Reflections on a Journey of Transformation,* documents the findings of that study but is not available for general distribution. A developing book on that project, *Midwifing the Organization,* edited by Gitti Jordan, is in progress and looking for a publisher. Readers seeking more information on ethnography should contact the Institute for Research on Learning in Menlo Park, California.

There are several good books on metaphor. *Metaphors We Live By,* by George Lakoff and Mark Johnson (University of Chicago, 1980), has been the standard for many years. Their new book, *Philosophy in the Flesh* (Basic Books, 1999), is a broader and deeper treatment of their thinking. I've also had many conversations with Colleen Burke about the use of metaphor in business and have visited Gerald Zaltman in his Harvard lab. Descriptions of the Zaltman metaphor-elicitation technique have appeared in *Fast Company, Fortune,* and other publications, but Zaltman's work is best understood in context. To explore this approach to analyzing living systems, contact Gerald Zaltman at Harvard Business School or Colleen Burke at cburke2@aol.com.

The principles of systems thinking are the heart of Peter Senge's *Fifth Discipline* (Doubleday/Currency, 1990). For readers looking to practice systems thinking, *The Systems Thinking Playbook,* by Linda Booth Sweeney and Dennis Meadows (Pegasus Communications, 1996), is a great resource. Practitioners will also find helpful ideas in *The Fifth Discipline Fieldbook* (Doubleday/Currency, 1994) and *The Dance of Change* (Doubleday/Currency, 1999), by Senge and friends.

The Living Company, by Arie de Geus (Harvard Business School Press, 1997), cannot be categorized as it includes ideas about living systems, scenario planning, and putting theory into action. However, it articulates beautifully the way people learn through discovery and play and is one of the most humane and least theoretical books around. Humberto Maturana's ideas and theories come from his book written with Francisco Varela, *The Tree of Knowledge* (Shambala, 1987), from numerous articles available on the Web, from a 1998 workshop with Maturana, and from our Maturana study group. *The Embodied Mind,* by Francisco Varela, Even Thompson, and Eleanor Rosch, is another good guide on the nature of cognition, although the prose is stilted.

The personal learning model used at XBS was researched, validated, and developed by Scheef Organizational Development and Training. The people/action/information styles are detailed in this approach. For more information, contact Devon Scheef at 100741.1010@compuserve.com. Other good sources on thinking and learning styles are *Thinking Styles,* by Robert J. Sternberg (Cambridge University Press, 1997), *Multiple Intelligences: The Theory in Practice,* by Howard Gardner (Basic Books, 1993), and Dawna Markova's *Art of the Possible* (Conari Press, 1991). My familiarity with D. A. Kolb's learning-styles inventory comes from personal experience, but his ideas are set forth in several of his works as well as on the Web. Robert Ornstein's *Right Mind* (Harcourt Brace, 1997) offers a well-researched and highly readable explanation of the differing roles of the right and left hemispheres of the brain. Principles about the social nature of learning have been researched and articulated by the Institute for Research on Learning. The story on Tom Snyder and his beliefs about on-line learning appeared in a *Boston Magazine* article titled "Laughing Matters" (September 1998). I have also had access to collaborative research on distance learning conducted by IRL and Sun Microsystems. Their findings are documented in *Rethinking "Distance" in Distance Learning* and can be requested from IRL. Information on corporate training expenditures came from the *Training Magazine* Web site. *The Power of Mindful Learning,* by Ellen J. Langer (Perseus Books, 1997), is highly recommended.

Research about the nature of competition, reward, and recognition is synthesized in Alfie Cohen's two books: *Punished by Rewards* (Houghton Mifflin, 1993) and *No Contest: The Case Against Competition* (Houghton Mifflin, 1986). *Readings About the Social Animal,* edited by Elliot Aronson (W. H. Freeman and Company, 1995), includes a selection of articles about humans and socials systems. The prisoner experiment described in Chapter 13 comes from the chapter titled "A Study of Prisoners and Guards in a Simulated Prison." Other interesting reports on the nature of conformity and obedience are included in this book.

Maverick, by Ricardo Semler, tells the story of a love-based organization—although he might not call it that—and *A Simpler Way,* by Meg Wheatley and Myron Kellner-Rogers (Barrett-Koehler, 1996), suggests how to go about creating humane environments. Ideas attributed to Dee Hock come out of our many and ongoing conversations about organizational paradox.

Many of the same sources were used for the chapters on patriarchy and diversity because the themes so often overlap. Although *The Protestant Ethic and the Spirit of Capitalism*, by Max Weber (Routledge, 1992), is dated, it continues to offer interesting perspectives. *Stratification and Power*, by John Scott (Polity Press, 1996), and *Engaging the Powers*, by Walter Wink (Fortress Press, 1992), are both good sources for understanding power structures. *The Alphabet Versus the Goddess*, by Leonard Schlain (Viking, 1998), is a history of patriarchy, human thought, and the conflict between word and image. It's highly readable and strongly recommended. Catharine MacKinnon's *Feminism Unmodified* (Harvard University Press, 1987) and Toni Morrison's *Playing in the Dark* (Vintage, 1993) are collections of lectures offering insights on power, feminism, and race.

The article about the new Alcoa headquarters, "And the Walls Came Tumbling Down," appeared in the December 13, 1998, issue of the *New York Times Magazine*. Bain's research on corporate programs appeared in the September 7, 1998, issue of *Fortune*. The story "A CEO Cuts His Own Pay" appeared in the October 26, 1998, issue of *Fortune*. The article about the new federal courthouse appeared in the *Boston Globe* on September 12, 1998. The Rosenbluth stories are drawn from *Good Company*, by Hal Rosenbluth and Diane McFerrin Peters (Addison-Wesley, 1998), and from conversations with people familiar with that organization. Chris Argyris has written numerous books that include his ideas about institutions and the importance of examining our own assumptions. *Knowledge for Action* (Josey-Bass, 1993) is an overview of Argyris's work and includes an explanation of the ladder of inference.

Ideas on diversity have also been informed by many works not mentioned in the text. *The Souls of Black Folk*, by W.E.B. DuBois (Bedford Books, 1996); *Invisible Man*, by Ralph Ellison (Vintage International, 1947); and *Beloved*, by Toni Morrison (Plume, 1988), are three of my favorites but there are many good narratives on what it means to be African American. *Africans in America*, by Charles Johnson, Patricia Smith, and the WGBH series research team (Harcourt Brace, 1998), written as companion to the recent PBS series, provides historical perspective. Cornel West's *Race Matters* (Vintage Books, 1994) is powerful.

The Hispanic Condition, by Ilan Stavans (HarperCollins, 1995), and *The Latino Condition*, edited by Richard Delgado and Jean Stefancic (New York University Press), are good introductory works, although my all-time pick is

The Milagro Beanfield War, by John Nichols (Ballantine Books, 1996). *Killing the White Man's Indian,* by Fergus Bordewich (Doubleday, 1996); *Neither Wolf nor Dog,* by Kent Nerburn (New World, 1994); and *Black Elk Speaks,* as told through John G. Neihardt (University of Nebraska Press, 1932), are also recommended, as are *Off White: Readings on Race, Power, and Society,* edited by Michelle Fine, Lois Weis, Linda C. Powell, and L. Mun Wong (Routledge, 1997), and Studs Terkel's *Race* (Doubleday, 1992).

There are also overlaps in the chapters on communication and staff work. *Selling the Invisible,* by Harry Beckwith (Warner Books, 1997), should be read by anyone with a service organization. It's short and right on. I also have relied frequently on *The New Positioning,* by Jack Trout (McGraw-Hill, 1996), and *Bottoms-Up Marketing,* by Al Ries and Jack Trout (Plume/Penguin, 1990). *Understanding Media,* by Marshall McLuhan (MIT Press, 1994), and *The Bias of Communication,* by Harold Innis (University of Toronto Press, 1995), have to be called seminal works—although I use that description sparingly. Innis's ideas about the role of media in the creation of history influenced McLuhan, who wrote thirty years ago about the emerging mass media, challenging conventional wisdom about how and what we communicate. I also enjoy Neil Postman's ideas—even though I don't always agree—detailed in *Technopoly* (Vintage, 1993), *Conscientious Objections* (Vintage, 1992), and *Amusing Ourselves to Death* (Penguin, 1986). *Language in Thought and Action,* by S. I. Hayakawa (Harcourt Brace, 1990); *The Structure of Magic,* vol. 2, by John Grinder and Richard Bandler (Science and Behavior Books, 1976); *The Rule of Metaphor,* by Paul Ricoeur (University of Toronto Press, 1977); and *Metaphor and Thought,* edited by Andrew Ortony (Cambridge University Press, 1993), all offer interesting perspectives on the interplay between language, thought, and action. *The Secret Language of Symbols,* by David Fontana (Chronicle Books, 1994); *The Dictionary of Symbolism,* by Hans Biedermann (Meridian, 1994); and *Envisioning Information,* by Edward R. Tufte (Graphic Press, 1990), illuminate how images and graphics can be used to animate communications. *Cross Cultural Design,* by Henry Steiner and Ken Haas (Thames and Hudson, 1995), is another good resource. The research on "conversation pieces" comes from *Communicating Change,* by T. J. and Sandar Larkin (McGraw Hill, 1994).

More ideas on sharing information and creating organizations of exceptional businesspeople can be found in *The Open-Book Experience,* by John Case (Perseus, 1998), and Jack Stack's *Great Game of Business* (Currency/Doubleday, 1992). There are a plethora of books on information, but my favorites include *Interface Culture,* by Steven Johnson (HarperEdge, 1997); *What Will Be,* by Michael Dertouzos (HarperEdge, 1997); *Data Smog,* by

David Shenk (HarperEdge, 1997); and *Life on the Screen,* by Sherry Turkle (Touchstone, 1995). "The Sorry Side of Sears" story appeared in the February 22, 1999, issue of *Newsweek.* The information on Zeller Electric came from conversations with Eric Zeller and visits to his company. The story of the Hollywood writer who passed herself off as a teenager appeared on *60 Minutes* in early 1999.

Vaclav Havel's *Open Letters: Selected Writings 1965–1990* (Vintage, 1992) contains his essay "The Power of the Powerless," and it appears again in a collection called *The Power of the Powerless* (M. E. Sharpe, 1985), which also contains Miroslav Kusy's essay "Chartism and 'Real Socialism.'" Other sources are Havel's *Disturbing the Peace* (Vintage, 1991) and *Summer Meditations* (Vintage, 1993).

The last chapter gallops across a big landscape and includes information from multiple sources. *The Buying of the Congress: How Special Interests Have Stolen Your Right to Life, Liberty, and the Pursuit of Happiness,* by Charles Lewis and the Center for Public Integrity (Avon Books, 1998), is a wonderful, well-researched resource on "the criminal class." The Center for Public Integrity is a nonpartisan, nonprofit group staffed by investigative reporters who have left major newspapers and television networks to research public service and ethics-related issues. Charles Lewis, the founder and executive director, did stints at ABC News and CBS News and was a producer for *60 Minutes.* This book is a must-read. Jim Hightower's *There's Nothing in the Middle of the Road but Yellow Stripes and Dead Armadillos* (HarperPerennial, 1997) is simultaneously hilarious and informative. *Biopiracy: The Plunder of Nature and Knowledge,* by Vandana Shiva (South End Press, 1997), exposes the dangers and inequities of the biotechnology industry. Shiva, whom I've also heard speak, is a physicist, an ecologist, and an activist and offers a powerful perspective for Western readers. *The Ethical Imperative: Why Moral Leadership Is Good Business,* by John Dalla Costa (Addison-Wesley, 1998), has proved extremely useful and is highly recommended. *Free Markets and Social Justice,* by Cass R. Sunstein (Oxford University Press, 1997), is dense and academic but contains wonderful information and ideas if you can plow through it. *Turbo Capitalism,* by Edward Luttwak (HarperCollins, 1999), is a good resource, as is David Korten's *Post-Corporate World* (Berrett-Koeher, 1999). *The Future of American Progressivism,* by Roberto Mangabeira Unger and Cornel West (Beacon Press, 1998), contains their proposal for mandatory voting. Background on Nelson Mandela came from his autobiography, *Long Walk to Freedom* (Little, Brown and Company, 1994). The Web also contains a wealth of information on Mandela, including his inaugural address. He attributes the inaugural quote to Marian Williamson.

"Even Executives Are Wincing at Executive Pay" appeared in the May 12, 1997, issue of *Business Week*. Peter Drucker's views on executives were contained in a March 10, 1997, *Forbes* article, "Seeing Things as They Really Are." The story about Bob Shapiro and Monsanto's culture appeared in the March 3,1999, *New York Times*. Voter turnout numbers came from the Associated Press story written November 6, 1996, by Deb Riechmann. *Time's* story on corporate welfare appeared in the November 9, 1998, issue. The social investment dollars quoted come from a research project sponsored by the Social Investment Forum and available on the Web. James Carville's ideas on campaign reform were proposed on several of his many television appearances. All numbers referenced in the last chapter come from the books and articles listed.

William Greider's *One World, Ready or Not: The Manic Logic of Global Capitalism* (Touchstone, 1997) and P. J. O'Rourke's *Eat the Rich* (Atlantic Monthly Press, 1998) are entertaining and insightful. Both authors write for *Rolling Stone* but, as politically polar opposites, see the world very differently. Also recommended is *The Biotech Century*, by Jeremy Rifkin (Jeremy P. Tarcher/Putnam, 1998).

Background books that undoubtedly contribute to the content include *Mind, Language, and Society*, by John Searle (Basic Books, 1998); Lani Guinier's *Lift Every Voice* (Simon & Schuster, 1998); *In Over Our Heads*, by Robert Kegan (Harvard University Press, 1994); *A History of Western Political Thought*, by J. S. McClelland (Routledge, 1996); Octavio Paz's *Labyrinth of Solitude* (Grove Press, 1985) and *One Earth, Four or Five Worlds: Reflections on Contemporary History* (Harcourt Brace, 1985). Additionally, Paz's 1990 Nobel Lecture is available on the Web. I also refer to ideas contained in *Emerson on Transcendentalism*, edited by Edward Ericson (Continuum, 1994), and *Walden and Civil Disobedience*, by Henry David Thoreau (Penguin Books, 1983), and my all-time favorite book on writing and life, *Bird by Bird*, by Anne Lamott (Anchor, 1995).

Index